Cooking with Mickey and the Chefs of Walt Disney World® Resort

Pam Brandon

A Roundtable Press Book

HYPERION
NEW YORK

W9-BAZ-542

A ROUNDTABLE PRESS BOOK

PRINTED IN CHINA

For information, address:
Hyperion, 114 Fifth Avenue, New York, NY 10011

For Hyperion
Editor: Wendy Lefkon
Assistant Editor: Robin Friedman

For Walt Disney World Attractions, Inc.
Product Developer: Tina Rebstock
Cover Design: David Whitaker

The editors would like to thank Thomas Belelieu, *Disney's Wine and Beverage Specialist*, and Karen Haynes in *Walt Disney World Food and Beverage*.

For Roundtable Press, Inc.
Directors: Susan E. Meyer, Marsha Melnick, Julie Merberg
Senior Editor: Carol Spier
Recipe Editor: Lori Longbotham
Book Design: Vertigo Design
Production: Bill Rose
Computer Production: Steven Rosen

ISBN 0-7868-6472-9

First Edition
2 4 6 8 10 9 7 5 3 1

Foreword

When it comes to food, millions of Walt Disney World guests are looking for everything from a scrumptious burger to impeccable gourmet cuisine. And when vacationers are back home in their own kitchens, many write or call to ask for a recipe that is part of their Disney vacation memories.

This cookbook offers some of those most-requested recipes from Walt Disney World® Resort and heralds a dramatic new chapter in Disney dining with new chefs, new restaurants, and more than 100 new recipes. Each recipe credits the creating chef and identifies the restaurant to help you remember—or know where to go for—an enjoyable meal.

Cooking with Mickey and the Chefs of Walt Disney World Resort is presented on a freestanding easel that makes it easy to use in the kitchen. You'll find chapters filled with nibbles, soups, breads, vegetables, seafood, meat and poultry, rice, pasta and grains, desserts, and of course, children's favorites. There are also recipes for complementary sauces and salad dressings, and an appendix of intense flavorings that enhance several of the dishes found elsewhere in the book.

Along with many of the recipes are wine suggestions from the Disney pros and tips from the chef instructors at the Disney Institute, a Walt Disney World resort that sponsors daily cooking classes for home chefs. And though the Disney chefs must cook for thousands, all of the recipes included here have been adapted to make family-size servings and were tested for home cooks.

We hope this exciting recipe collection helps you re-create vacation memories at home—and most of all, we invite you back to our table, to experience the delightful cuisine prepared by the Walt Disney World chefs.

Cooking with Mickey and the Chefs of Walt Disney World® Resort

Contents

Contents

Contents

Introduction

"There is no greater love than the love of food," wrote George Bernard Shaw. Air and water give us life, but food gives us a way of life.

As we approach the millennium, the Walt Disney World® Resort has created many customized dining destinations that stimulate all of the senses and please diverse palates. Stylish, relaxed restaurant settings feature open kitchens, exposed wine cellars, and, the stars of the show—superlative food and excellent service.

Delivering great food and great service takes great people. The Walt Disney World chefs are passionate about what they do and what they believe, teaming up with restaurant managers to show off their creativity and knowledge, and to take care of the guests. Our chefs come from all corners of the world, with different cooking styles and cultural backgrounds influencing their creativity. As a result, the diverse Disney restaurants are a reflection of myriad influences and celebrate a cuisine with almost no rules or regulations: As long as the food looks appealing and tastes delicious, almost anything goes.

It takes a lot of people to create this free spirit, and that really adds to the beauty of the dining experience here. You can't get too serious—open, young minds do not always adhere to the classical rules. Instead, passionate cooks base their work on their palates and what is in the market. For them, cooking is not just a job, it's a lifestyle, a reflection of themselves.

Today's cuisine is made rich by our amazing accessibility to food from around the world: beautiful sea bass from Seattle, ripe papayas from Hawaii, smoked hams from Virginia, heirloom tomatoes from California, live lobsters from Maine. Freshness is the key. And as you create meals in your own home, it is also important to enjoy local farmers' markets and any produce that may grow in your own backyard. The cycle of planting, growing, harvesting, and feasting is good for the soul and enhances your personal lifestyle.

This all-new edition of *Cooking with Mickey and the Chefs of Walt Disney World Resort* offers updated recipes for you to try at home—recipes that we hope are mostly easy and, even when challenging, fun to prepare and delicious to eat. Tips and short-cuts from the Disney Institute chefs will help guide you through some of the more challenging dishes.

Thank you for returning time and again to Walt Disney World® Resort. We hope that you have a lot of enjoyable meals here...and if you haven't experienced Disney, now is the time!

Dieter Hannig
Vice President of Food and Beverage
Walt Disney World Resort

Nibbles

Smoked Salmon Spread

Chef Robert Adams,
Artist Point

Serves 6 to 8 as an appetizer; makes about 1 ½ cups.

Once you've prepared this recipe and have learned how to smoke your own fish, it may become your favorite way to serve fish as an entrée as well as an appetizer.

2 **cups wood chips**

6 **ounces fresh tuna steak**

6 **ounces fresh salmon steak**

Salt and freshly ground pepper to taste

2 **tablespoons pure maple syrup**

¼ **cup (½ stick) butter, softened**

2 **tablespoons heavy cream**

1 **teaspoon lemon juice, or to taste**

½ **teaspoon drained prepared horseradish**

2 **drops Tabasco sauce, or to taste**

1 **teaspoon snipped fresh chives**

Assorted warm breads and crackers for serving

1. In a large bowl, place the wood chips in water to cover. Soak at least 4 hours but preferably overnight.

2. Drain the wood chips thoroughly and place them in the center of a 24-inch by 18-inch piece of heavy-duty aluminum foil. Fold the foil to form a square pouch, sealing the edges securely. With a barbecue fork, poke about 20 large holes on one side of pouch for the smoke to escape.

3. For a charcoal grill, place the coals to one side of your grill, light, and wait until the coals start to show a light layer of white ash. For a gas grill, preheat one side to medium.

4. Place the pouch of wood chips directly on the coals or lava rocks with the holes facing up. If you are using a gas grill, reduce the temperature to low at this point. ☞

5. Place the tuna and the salmon on the cold side of the grill (use aluminum foil to support the fish if needed), and season with salt and pepper.

6. Close the lid and smoke the fish until golden brown and cooked through; depending on the size of your fish and the heat of your grill, it will take at least 45 minutes and up to 1 hour.

7. Brush the fish with the maple syrup and remove from the grill.

8. Let the fish cool slightly. Remove the skin, place the fish in a food processor, and puree until smooth. Add the butter, heavy cream, lemon juice, horseradish, salt and pepper to taste, and Tabasco sauce and puree until smooth.

9. Transfer the spread to a small serving bowl and garnish with chives. Serve warm or at room temperature with breads and crackers.

Disney Institute Tip: Any variety of wood chip is suitable for smoking; cherry is used at Artist Point. Use caution when disposing of the chip pouch—it is advisable to submerse the pouch in water until cool.

The Wine Steward Suggests: Acidity to counteract the "fatness" of the salmon must be a key ingredient in an accompanying wine. Additionally, you'll want a varietal that will allow the smokiness and woodiness of the spread to stay in the foreground. We recommend a Sauvignon Blanc—its light touch of oak will match the smoky flavor, and its delicate herbal notes will complement it.

Hitipi

Chef Bart Hosmer,
Spoodles

Serves 6 to 8; makes about 1⅔ cups.

Hitipi does exactly what an appetizer should do: increase your appetite for the meal to come. Use nonfat yogurt and reduced-fat sour cream, if you prefer.

- 1½ cups crumbled feta cheese (about 8 ounces)
- ½ cup plain yogurt
- ½ cup sour cream
- 1 teaspoon minced garlic
- ¼ teaspoon salt, or to taste
- ¼ teaspoon freshly ground black pepper, or to taste

  Pita bread for serving, warmed and cut into triangles

1. In a blender or a food processor, puree the feta, yogurt, sour cream, garlic, salt, and pepper until smooth.
2. Transfer the mixture to a serving bowl and serve as a spread or a dip with the warm pita bread.

Disney Institute Tip: If you feel the urge, add minced fresh herbs to the Hitipi. Mint, dill, parsley, and/or basil would all be terrific.

Mango Salsa

Chef Michael Bersell,
Captain's Tavern

Serves 2 to 4; makes about 2 cups.

When mangoes are plentiful, this simple, fresh combination makes a zesty dip for tortilla chips—you may never go back to tomato salsas!

2 ripe mangoes

2 scallions, finely chopped

3 tablespoons lime juice, preferably **Key** lime juice

1 tablespoon finely chopped peeled fresh ginger

1 tablespoon light brown sugar

¼ teaspoon salt, or to taste

A pinch freshly ground pepper, or to taste

Tortilla chips for serving

1. Peel, seed, and chop the mangoes.

2. In a serving bowl, stir together the mango, scallions, lime juice, ginger, brown sugar, salt, and pepper until thoroughly combined.

3. Serve as a nibble with tortilla chips.

Disney Institute Tip: Use this salsa as a very quick and easy sauce for grilled or broiled fish, poultry, or pork.

Vegetable Cream Cheese

Chef David Hoffman,
Yacht Club Galley

Serves 4 to 6; makes a generous 1 cup.

Serve this to your family and friends for a little nibble before dinner—it's great with a glass of white wine.

8 ounces cream cheese, softened

¼ cup chopped fresh parsley

2 tablespoons **Knorr Swiss Vegetable Soup Mix**

A pinch freshly ground pepper, or to taste

A pinch Spike seasoning or other spicy salt-free seasoning

1. In a medium bowl, with a fork, whip the cream cheese until soft and fluffy.

2. Add the parsley, Knorr Swiss Vegetable Soup Mix, black pepper, and Spike seasoning and stir to blend completely.

3. Let the spread sit at room temperature for at least 1 to 2 hours to allow the soup mix vegetables to soften and the flavors to develop.

4. Serve at room temperature or slightly chilled.

Disney Institute Tip: This quick and easy spread was designed as the perfect accompaniment to the Cobblestone Cheese Bread on page 41. It's equally tasty with crackers or croutons.

Red Pepper Sauce

Chef Darryl Mickler,
Disney-MGM Studios
Catering

Makes about 1½ cups.

Modeled on a classic Middle Eastern dish called Muhammara, this delicious spread and/or dip has a very complex, unusual, and interesting flavor. You'll find tons of uses for it, once you've tasted it.

½ cup coarsely chopped walnuts

1 tablespoon soft fresh bread crumbs

2 roasted red bell peppers, peeled, seeded, and chopped

1 arbol chile, reconstituted, drained, and minced, or ⅛ teaspoon cayenne pepper, or to taste

3 tablespoons fresh lemon juice

1 tablespoon plus 1 teaspoon pomegranate molasses

1 tablespoon extra-virgin olive oil

½ teaspoon ground cumin seed

¼ teaspoon salt, or to taste

⅛ teaspoon freshly ground pepper, or to taste

1. In a food processor, finely chop the walnuts with the bread crumbs.

2. Add the bell peppers and puree.

3. Add the arbol chile, lemon juice, pomegranate molasses, olive oil, cumin, salt, and pepper and puree.

4. If not using immediately, store covered and chilled until ready to serve. Can be made 1 to 2 days ahead.

Disney Institute Tip: Pomegranate molasses can be purchased in many specialty food stores, by mail order, and in Middle Eastern markets. Since it keeps almost indefinitely in the refrigerator and adds a unique tart and sweet flavor, it's great to have on hand.

Yogurt and Boursin Spread

Chef Darryl Mickler,
Disney-MGM Studios
Catering

Makes about ⅔ cup.

Here's a delightful alternative to mustard or mayonnaise on almost any sandwich. The refreshing blend of flavors is especially delicious on the Grilled Eggplant Sandwich, page 65.

⅔ cup plain yogurt

⅓ cup garlic- and herb-flavored Boursin cheese, at room temperature

1 teaspoon minced fresh mint leaves, or to taste

½ teaspoon finely grated lemon zest

¼ teaspoon salt, or to taste

⅛ teaspoon freshly ground pepper, or to taste

1. In a strainer lined with a double layer of damp cheesecloth, drain the yogurt for 20 minutes. Discard the liquid.

2. In a small bowl, combine the Boursin cheese with the yogurt until smooth and well blended.

3. Stir in the minced fresh mint, lemon zest, salt, and pepper until well combined.

4. If not using immediately, store covered and chilled until ready to serve. Can be made 1 to 2 days ahead.

Disney Institute Tip: In Middle Eastern cuisines the strained yogurt made in step 1 is called *leban*. It is used as an appetizer and as an ingredient in many dishes. You can use it in the same way you'd use cream cheese.

Gorgonzola and Golden Onion Tart

Chef Michael LaDuke,
The Hollywood Brown
Derby

Serves 8.

Guests at The
Hollywood Brown
Derby frequently
request this recipe.
The versatile tart can
accompany a meat or
fish entrée, be served
alone as a rich hors
d'oeuvre, or become a
light entrée along with a
cool green salad.

- **2** slices bacon, cut into ½-inch pieces
- **2** cups thinly sliced onions
- **2** large potatoes, peeled and coarsely grated
- **1** cup coarsely grated Swiss cheese
- **1** cup crumbled Gorgonzola cheese
- **¼** cup snipped fresh chives
- **¾** teaspoon salt, or to taste
- **¼** teaspoon freshly ground pepper, or to taste
- **1** cup heavy cream
- **2** large eggs, lightly beaten

1. Preheat the oven to 350°F.

2. In a 10- to 12-inch skillet, cook the bacon, stirring, over medium heat until translucent. Stir in the onions and cook, stirring, for 12 to 15 minutes, or until golden brown. With a slotted spoon, transfer the bacon and onion mixture to paper towels to drain.

3. In a large mixing bowl, stir together the bacon mixture, potatoes, Swiss cheese, Gorgonzola cheese, chives, salt, and pepper until well combined.

4. In a small bowl, with a fork, combine the cream and the eggs and fold into the potato mixture.

5. Place the mixture in a lightly oiled 10-inch pie plate. Cover the dish with aluminum foil and bake for 30 minutes. Remove the foil and bake uncovered for 15 minutes longer. Cut into 8 wedges and serve hot.

The Wine Steward Suggests: This tart offers exciting opposing flavors. For a wine that balances the sweetness of the onions with lush fruitiness, try a Pinot Grigio.

Crab and Roasted Corn Quesadilla

Chef Michael LaDuke,
The Hollywood Brown
Derby

Serves 4.

The roasted corn lends a distinctive flavor to this popular appetizer. Serve the wedges with a dollop of sour cream and tomato salsa.

2 cups corn kernels, preferably fresh

1 tablespoon vegetable oil

1 teaspoon chili powder

¼ cup finely diced red pepper

¼ cup finely diced red onion

3 tablespoons chopped cilantro

1 teaspoon finely chopped canned chipotle chiles in adobo, or to taste

1 cup fresh lump crabmeat, picked over

1 cup coarsely grated Monterey Jack cheese

Eight 8-inch flour tortillas

1 ripe tomato, chopped

1 tablespoon lime juice

1 cup favorite homemade or store-bought tomato salsa

1. Preheat the oven to 350°F.

2. On a baking sheet, toss together the corn, oil, and chili powder. With a spatula, spread the mixture evenly. Roast the corn for 10 minutes.

3. Transfer the corn to a bowl and combine with the red pepper, red onion, 2 tablespoons of the cilantro, and the chipotle.

4. In a bowl, combine ½ cup of the corn mixture, the crabmeat, and the grated Monterey Jack cheese.

5. On a work surface, lay out 4 tortillas. Evenly divide the crab mixture on the tortillas, using about ½ cup for each. Top with the remaining 4 tortillas.

6. In a small bowl, combine the remaining corn salsa with the tomato, lime juice, and the remaining 1 tablespoon cilantro.

☞

7. On the lightly oiled rack of a grill over glowing coals or on a ridged stove-top grill pan heated over medium heat, grill the tortillas, in batches if necessary, until golden brown on both sides.

8. Cut the quesadillas into wedges, transfer to serving plates, and serve hot with the tomato salsa and the corn salsa.

Disney Institute Tip: If you're firing up your grill for this recipe, you can choose to grill rather than roast the corn. Leave the kernels on the cob, brush them with oil, sprinkle with chili powder, and grill until nicely browned. When the corn is cool enough to handle, remove the kernels with a sharp knife.

The Wine Steward Suggests: Crab and Roast Corn Quesadilla offers your palate a real variety of savory sensations. To calm things down, serve a wine with a solid and "dependable" flavor—a Pinot Blanc is a splendid match to seafood and always seems to keep the tastebuds on the right track.

Moroccan Spiced Tuna Salad

Chef Bart Hosmer,
Spoodles

Serves 4.

This Mediterranean-style creation is one of the favorite dishes for sharing at Spoodles. Make it easy on yourself when you shave the Pecorino—let the cheese come to room temperature and use a sharp vegetable peeler.

2   tablespoons Ras el Hanout spice mixture (recipe page 164)

    Four ¾-inch thick tuna steaks

3   tablespoons olive oil

1   medium fennel bulb, sliced paper-thin (about 4 cups)

2   tablespoons fresh lemon juice

¼   teaspoon salt, or to taste

A pinch freshly ground pepper, or to taste

¼   cup thinly sliced quartered red onion

2   tablespoons 1-inch pieces fresh chives

1   tablespoon drained capers

¼   cup Pecorino Romano cheese shaved with a vegetable peeler

1. On a dinner plate, sprinkle the Ras el Hanout. Coat the tuna on all sides.

2. In a 12-inch skillet, heat 2 tablespoons of the olive oil over medium-high heat until hot but not smoking. Cook the tuna, turning to cook all sides, 7 to 8 minutes for rare, or to desired doneness. Transfer the tuna to a platter, let come to room temperature, and chill, covered, until cold, about 1 hour.

3. In a bowl, stir together the fennel, lemon juice, remaining 1 tablespoon olive oil, salt, and pepper; toss gently.

4. When ready to serve, pile the fennel on 4 chilled serving plates for height. Slice the tuna into ½-inch thick slices and arrange around the fennel salad.

5. Garnish the salad with the red onion, chives, capers, and finally with the Pecorino shavings.

Red Snapper Carpaccio with Bell Pepper— Melon Salsa

Chef Roland Muller,
Cítricos

Serves 2.

Sweet honeydew and crunchy peppers combined with wafer-thin raw snapper make a refreshing summer starter.

One 4-ounce skinless fresh red snapper filet

3 tablespoons fresh lime juice, plus additional for mixed greens, if desired

¼ teaspoon salt, or to taste

⅛ teaspoon freshly ground pepper, or to taste

¼ cup finely diced honeydew melon

¼ cup finely diced green bell pepper

¼ cup finely diced red bell pepper

¼ cup finely diced yellow bell pepper

¼ cup finely diced red onion

2 tablespoons olive oil

1 tablespoon chopped cilantro

A pinch crushed hot red pepper flakes

2 cups mixed greens such as mesclun for serving (optional)

1. With a sharp knife, slice the filet into 4 small medallions, each weighing about 1 ounce. Lightly oil two 6-inch by 6-inch squares of parchment or wax paper. Place the medallions on one piece of the parchment paper and cover with the remaining piece. Gently pound the fish with the smooth side of a mallet or with the bottom of a saucepan until the medallions are as thin as possible without tearing.

2. On two chilled, lightly oiled plates, arrange the fish, removing the paper. Drizzle the fish with 1 tablespoon of the lime juice and season with ⅛ teaspoon salt and a pinch of freshly ground pepper. Marinate the red snapper, covered and chilled, for six to eight hours. ☞

3. Meanwhile, combine the honeydew, green, red, and yellow bell peppers, onion, olive oil, remaining 2 tablespoons lime juice, cilantro, remaining ⅛ teaspoon salt, a pinch of freshly ground pepper, and the red pepper flakes. Taste and adjust the seasonings. Cover and chill until ready to serve.

4. Just before serving, remove the plates from the refrigerator and garnish each piece of fish with the Bell Pepper–Melon Salsa. Place a small amount of mixed greens in the center of each plate, sprinkle with freshly ground pepper, and add a squeeze of fresh lime juice, if desired.

Disney Institute Tip: Use the freshest red snapper available for this dish. If you'd like to make 4 servings, the recipe can easily be doubled.

Salmon Tartare with Fennel Salad

Chef Roland Muller,
Cítricos

Serves 4.

Start with extremely fresh salmon to make this elegant appetizer. The acidity of the lime juice "cooks" the salmon to a delicate, melt-in-your-mouth texture.

14 ounces skinless fresh salmon filet, cut into ½-inch dice

½ cup finely diced fennel

½ cup finely diced shallots

1 tablespoon fresh lime juice

1 tablespoon olive oil

1 tablespoon minced fresh dill

½ teaspoon salt, or to taste

A pinch freshly ground pepper, or to taste

A pinch crushed hot red pepper flakes

1 fennel bulb, trimmed and very thinly shaved (about 4 cups)

¼ cup balsamic vinegar

¼ cup olive oil

¼ teaspoon salt, or to taste

⅛ teaspoon freshly ground pepper, or to taste

1. In a medium bowl, combine the salmon, diced fennel, shallots, lime juice, olive oil, dill, salt, freshly ground pepper, and hot red pepper flakes. Taste and adjust seasoning. Cover and chill until ready to serve.

2. In a medium bowl, combine the shaved fennel, balsamic vinegar, olive oil, salt, and pepper. Taste and adjust seasoning. Cover and chill until ready to serve.

3. To serve, arrange the fennel salad on 4 chilled serving plates and top with the salmon tartare. Serve immediately.

Soups

New England Clam Chowder

Chef Barry Fisher,
Cape May Cafe

Serves 8 as a first course or 4 as a main course; makes about 8 cups.

On a visit to Cape May, New Jersey, the chef collected this original recipe for "white" clam chowder.

½ cup (1 stick) butter

⅓ cup all-purpose flour

2 tablespoons vegetable oil

1 large onion, finely chopped

3 stalks celery, finely chopped

2 cups clam broth

3 medium-sized red potatoes, cut into ½-inch dice (about 3 cups)

Two 6½-ounce cans chopped clams, liquid reserved

1 teaspoon dried thyme leaves, crumbled

½ teaspoon dried basil leaves, crumbled

½ teaspoon salt, or to taste

¼ teaspoon freshly ground pepper, or to taste

4 drops Tabasco sauce, or to taste

2 cups half-and-half

1. In a 2-quart saucepan, melt the butter over medium heat. Add the flour and cook, stirring constantly, for 3 minutes. Remove the saucepan from the heat and set aside.

2. In a 4- to 5-quart Dutch oven, heat the oil over medium heat until hot but not smoking. Add the onion and the celery and cook, stirring, until the onion is softened, about 5 minutes.

3. Stir in the clam broth, potatoes, chopped clams with their liquid, thyme, basil, salt, pepper, and Tabasco sauce. Bring the mixture to a simmer over medium heat and simmer for 5 minutes, or until the potatoes are cooked through.

4. Add the half-and-half and bring to a low boil over medium-high heat. Slowly add the butter and flour mixture, whisking constantly, until well blended. Reduce the heat to low and simmer the soup for 10 minutes, stirring occasionally.

White Onion Soup

Chef Robert Adams,
Artist Point

Serves 4; makes about 3¼ cups.

If you prefer, toast a slice of French or Italian bread, melt some Pecorino Romano cheese on top, and sprinkle with chives and place it in the soup as a garnish.

- **¼ cup (½ stick) butter**
- **3 medium-sized white onions, cut into ¼-inch dice**
- **2 cups low-sodium chicken broth or stock, preferably homemade**
- **½ teaspoon salt, or to taste**
- **A pinch freshly ground white pepper**
- **½ cup sour cream**
- **Snipped fresh chives or chopped fresh parsley for garnish**

1. In a 4- to 5-quart Dutch oven, melt the butter over low heat. Add the onions and cook, stirring frequently, for 45 minutes; do not let the onions brown.

2. In a food processor, puree the onions until smooth.

3. Return the onions to the Dutch oven and whisk in the chicken broth, salt, and pepper.

4. Remove 2 cups of the onion mixture to a bowl and whisk in the sour cream.

5. Whisking constantly, return the sour cream mixture to the soup and heat through; do not let the soup boil.

6. Serve the soup hot, garnished with the snipped fresh chives.

Lamb and Barley Soup

Chef Philippe Cuenin,
Rose & Crown
Pub & Dining Room

**Serves 6 to 8
as a first course
or 4 as a main course;
makes about 9 cups.**

British visitors (especially Scots) feel right at home when they sit down to a steaming bowl of this soup at the United Kingdom Pavilion at Epcot. The chef added fresh basil—not at all traditional, but quite delicious.

- **1** cup barley
- **12** ounces ground lamb
- **2** tablespoons canola or other vegetable oil
- **1** onion, finely chopped
- **1** garlic clove, minced
- **2** tablespoons all-purpose flour
- **5** cups chicken broth
- **¾** cup milk
- **3** stalks celery, trimmed and finely chopped
- **2** medium carrots, peeled and finely chopped
- **1** medium turnip, peeled and finely chopped
- **6** tablespoons finely shredded fresh basil leaves or minced fresh parsley
- **1** teaspoon salt, or to taste
- **¼** teaspoon freshly ground pepper, or to taste

1. In a large pot of boiling salted water, cook the barley for 30 minutes, or according to the package directions. Drain completely in a colander and set aside.

2. Meanwhile, in a 4- to 5-quart Dutch oven, cook the ground lamb over medium heat, stirring and breaking up the lamb with a spoon, for about 6 to 8 minutes, or until it is cooked through and no pinkness remains. With a slotted spoon, transfer the lamb to towels to drain. Pour off and discard any remaining fat.

3. In the same Dutch oven, heat the canola oil over medium heat until hot but not smoking. Add the onion and the garlic and cook, stirring, about 5 minutes, or until the onion is softened. Stir in the flour and cook, stirring constantly, until lightly browned, about 5 minutes. ☞

4. Add the chicken broth and bring the mixture to a boil. Reduce the heat and simmer for 15 minutes. Add the cooked barley, milk, celery, carrots, turnip, ¼ cup fresh basil, salt, and pepper and cook, stirring occasionally, until the vegetables are tender, about 25 minutes.

5. Serve the soup hot, garnished with the remaining 2 tablespoons fresh basil.

Boatwright's Crab Soup

Chef Michael Deardorff,
Boatwright's Dining Hall

Serves 6 to 8; makes about 6 cups.

Standard fare in many parts of the South, this rich crab soup becomes a satisfying meal when served with a tossed green salad and oyster crackers.

2 cups heavy cream

1 pint half-and-half

1 cup milk

1 cup finely diced potatoes

1 cup finely diced carrots

½ pound lump crabmeat, picked over

½ cup corn kernels, preferably fresh

½ teaspoon salt, or to taste

¼ teaspoon freshly ground pepper, or to taste

¼ cup water

1 tablespoon cornstarch

1 cup clam broth

2 tablespoons finely chopped scallions

1 tablespoon minced fresh dill

1 tablespoon Pernod

1. In a 4- or 5-quart Dutch oven, heat the heavy cream, half-and-half, and milk to a simmer over medium heat.

2. Add the potatoes, carrots, crabmeat, corn, salt, and pepper. Reduce the heat to low and simmer, stirring occasionally, until the vegetables are softened, about 15 minutes.

3. In a small bowl, whisk together the water and the cornstarch. Add the cornstarch mixture and the clam broth to the cream mixture and bring to a boil, stirring constantly. Boil for 1 minute, or until thickened.

4. Just before serving, stir in the scallions, dill, and Pernod.

Cashew Cream Soup

Chef Scott Hunnel,
Victoria & Albert's

Serves 4 to 6; makes about 6 cups.

This unusual combination of flavors makes a rich, sweet beginning for a special meal.

- **2 tablespoons oil, preferably walnut oil**
- **2 cups raw cashew nuts plus additional coarsely chopped for garnish**
- **1 cup chopped onion**
- **¾ cup chopped carrots**
- **¾ cup chopped celery**
- **1 teaspoon minced garlic**
- **¼ cup Amaretto (optional)**
- **5 cups heavy cream**
- **4 cups chicken broth**
- **1 teaspoon salt, or to taste**
- **¼ teaspoon freshly ground pepper, or to taste**

1. In a 4- to 5-quart Dutch oven, heat the oil over medium heat. Add the cashews and cook, stirring, for 5 to 6 minutes, or until the cashews begin to brown. Add the onion, carrots, celery, and garlic and cook, stirring, for 5 to 6 minutes, or until the vegetables are softened.

2. Add the Amaretto, if using, and simmer for 1 minute. Stir in the heavy cream and the chicken broth and simmer, covered, stirring occasionally, for about 30 minutes or until the vegetables are softened and the soup has thickened slightly. Remove the Dutch oven from the heat.

3. Puree the soup with an immersion blender or in a regular blender in batches.

4. Strain the soup through a fine sieve and season with salt and pepper. Serve the soup hot, garnished with the remaining chopped cashew nuts.

Disney Institute Tip: Add a squeeze of lemon and a dash of Tasbasco sauce to really perk up the flavor.

Oyster-Brie Soup

Chef Michael LaDuke,
The Hollywood Brown Derby

Serves 4 to 6; makes about 5 cups.

Requests for this Hollywood Brown Derby specialty are so frequent that Chef Michael LaDuke has it printed on recipe-card-sized derby hats, ready to hand to guests.

3 tablespoons butter

3 tablespoons all-purpose flour

2 pints half-and-half

6 ounces Brie cheese, cut into 1-inch cubes

4 cups clam broth

8 ounces shucked oysters with their liqueur

¾ cup Champagne or dry white wine

½ teaspoon salt, or to taste

¼ teaspoon freshly ground pepper, or to taste

Fresh dill sprigs for garnish

1. In a 2-quart saucepan, melt the butter over medium heat. To make a roux, add the flour and cook, stirring constantly, for 2 to 3 minutes, or just long enough to cook the raw flavor out of the flour. Using a rubber spatula, transfer the roux to a bowl; let it cool, uncovered, to room temperature.

2. In a 4- or 5-quart Dutch oven, bring the half-and-half just to boiling over medium-high heat. Reduce the heat to the lowest possible setting and add the cooled roux, whisking until smooth. Simmer the mixture, stirring, for 7 to 8 minutes, or until thickened.

3. Add the Brie and cook, stirring or whisking constantly, until the cheese is melted and smooth.

4. Stir in the clam broth. Strain the mixture through a coarse sieve and return it to the cleaned Dutch oven; discard the solids. ☞

5. In a small skillet, cook the oysters in their liqueur over medium heat, just until the edges begin to curl. Add the oysters and the Champagne to the cheese mixture. Strain the oyster liqueur through a coarse sieve lined with damp paper towels into the cheese mixture. Season with salt and pepper.

6. Serve the soup hot, garnished with dill sprigs.

Disney Institute Tip: Don't remove the rind from the cheese when cutting it into cubes, it's perfectly edible.

Conch Chowder

Chef Michael Schifano,
Olivia's Cafe

Serves 8 to 10; makes about 8 cups.

Conch has a clamlike taste and a chewy texture; serve with a splash of hot sauce for a true taste of Southern Florida and the Bahamas.

1 pound fresh or thawed frozen conch meat

4 slices bacon, cut into ½-inch pieces

1 medium onion, cut into ½-inch dice

2 large ribs celery, coarsely diced

½ cup coarsely diced green bell pepper

½ cup coarsely diced red bell pepper

1 garlic clove, minced

¼ cup dry sherry

4 cups water

3 cups clam broth

One 28-ounce can diced tomatoes

½ cup tomato puree

1 large potato, peeled and cut into ½-inch dice

1. In a food processor, coarsely chop the conch meat.

2. In a 4- to 5-quart Dutch oven, cook the bacon over medium heat, stirring, 5 to 6 minutes, or until browned. With a slotted spoon, transfer the bacon to paper towels to drain.

3. Add the onion, celery, green bell pepper, red bell pepper, and garlic and cook, stirring, for 5 minutes. Add the sherry and cook for 1 minute. Stir in the conch meat, water, clam broth, canned tomatoes, and tomato puree and simmer, stirring occasionally, for 30 minutes. Add the potatoes and the bacon and cook, stirring occasionally, for 20 minutes.

4. Serve hot.

Disney Institute Tip: If fresh conch isn't available, frozen conch, available at many fish markets, works fine.

Canadian Cheddar Cheese Soup

Chef Gary Patterson,
Le Cellier Steakhouse

Serves 4 to 6; makes about 4 cups.

Tabasco and Worcestershire sauces add zing to a creamy soup that makes a satisfying supper when served with a salad on a cool fall or winter evening.

- 3 cups milk
- 1 cup chicken broth
- 6 slices bacon, diced
- ¼ cup finely diced red onion
- ¼ cup finely diced celery
- ¼ cup chopped scallion
- 3 tablespoons all-purpose flour
- 2 cups shredded Canadian white cheddar cheese
- ½ teaspoon Tabasco sauce, or to taste
- ½ teaspoon Worcestershire sauce
- ½ teaspoon salt, or to taste
- ⅛ teaspoon freshly ground pepper, or to taste

  Snipped fresh chives or minced scallions for garnish

1. In a 2-quart saucepan, heat the milk and the chicken broth over medium-low heat.

2. Meanwhile, in a 4- or 5-quart Dutch oven, cook the bacon, stirring, over medium heat for about 5 minutes, or until lightly browned.

3. Add the red onion, celery, and scallion and cook, stirring, until the onion has softened, about 5 minutes. Add the flour and cook, stirring constantly, for 3 minutes.

4. Remove the Dutch oven from the heat, add the heated milk mixture, and whisk until well blended. Return to the heat and cook, whisking constantly, until the mixture comes to a boil. Boil for 1 minute, or until thickened.

5. Remove the Dutch oven from the heat and stir in the cheese, Tabasco sauce, Worcestershire sauce, salt, and pepper until the cheese is melted and the soup is smooth.

6. Serve the soup hot, garnished with chives.

Breads

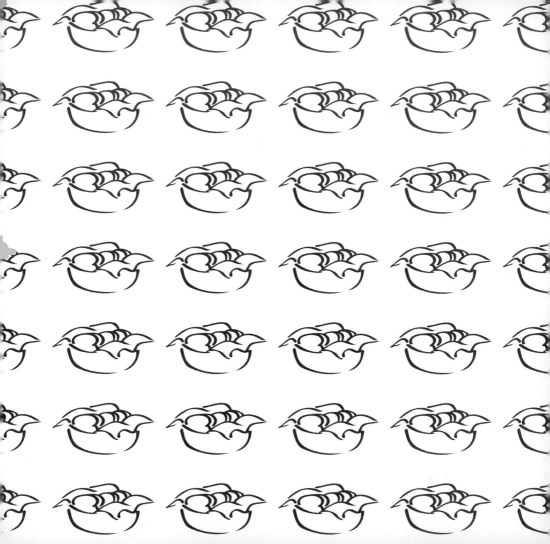

Cobblestone Cheese Bread

Chef David Hoffman,
Yacht Club Galley

Makes 2 loaves.

When it is served warm with Vegetable Cream Cheese (recipe, page 17), this bread quickly disappears from the tables of the Yacht Club Galley at Disney's Yacht & Beach Club Resort.

2 cups coarsely grated cheddar cheese

1 ½ cups water

½ oup milk

5 cups bread flour

¼ cup granulated sugar

2 tablespoons butter or margarine, melted and cooled

Two ¼-ounce packages active dry yeast

1 tablespoon salt

1. Place the grated cheese, tightly wrapped, in the freezer for 1 hour before beginning to make the bread.

2. In a 2-quart saucepan, heat the water and the milk over medium-low heat to 105°F to 115°F.

3. In the large bowl of an electric mixer, place the milk mixture, flour, sugar, butter, yeast, and salt. With the dough hook, beat the mixture on medium-high speed 5 to 6 minutes, or until the dough pulls away from the side of the bowl.

4. With the mixer on low speed, add 1½ cups of the cheese to the bread dough and beat until the cheese is well combined.

5. Lightly grease two 8½-inch by 4½-inch loaf pans. Divide the dough in half, lightly knead each half until smooth, and shape into 2 loaves. Transfer the dough to the prepared pans and divide the remaining ½ cup of cheese over the tops. Set the pans in a warm place, cover with a towel, and let rise about 1 hour, or until doubled in size.

6. Preheat the oven to 350°F.

7. Bake for 25 to 30 minutes, or until golden brown. Cool bread on a rack before serving.

Potato Bread

Chef Philippe Cuenin,
Rose & Crown
Pub & Dining Room

Makes 2 loaves.

This British recipe is served in mini-loaves at the Rose & Crown in the United Kingdom Pavilion at Epcot.

5 cups all-purpose flour, or as needed

1½ cups instant mashed potato flakes

1 tablespoon salt

2 teaspoons sugar

Two ¼-ounce packages active dry yeast

1½ cups water

1 cup milk

¼ cup vegetable oil

1. In the large bowl of an electric mixer, with the dough hook, combine the flour, the potato flakes, salt, sugar, and yeast.

2. In a 3-quart saucepan, heat the water and the milk over medium heat to 105°F to 115°F. Remove the saucepan from the heat and add the vegetable oil.

3. Add the water mixture to the dry ingredients and use the dough hook to combine. Continue kneading with the dough hook for 5 minutes, adding up to ¼ cup flour if the dough is too sticky.

4. On a lightly floured surface, knead the dough for about 1 minute, to form a smooth ball. Transfer the dough to a large, lightly oiled bowl, cover with a cloth, and set aside to rise in a warm place for 1 to 1½ hours, or until doubled in size.

5. Lightly grease two 9-inch by 5-inch loaf pans. ☞

6. On a lightly floured surface, punch down the dough and knead for 1 minute. Divide the dough in half and shape each piece into a 7-inch by 4-inch loaf. Transfer the loaves to the prepared pans, and slash 3 even cuts on the top of each loaf with a knife. Cover with a cloth and set the loaves aside in a warm place for about 1 hour, or until doubled in size.

7. Preheat the oven to 375°F.

8. Bake for 25 to 30 minutes, or until the loaves are golden brown and sound hollow when tapped on the bottom. Turn out immediately and cool on wire racks.

Flax Seed Bread

Chef Erich Herbitschek,
Disney's Grand Floridian
Resort & Spa Bakery

Serves 4 to 8.

Hearty and healthful, flax seed bread gets raves at Narcoossee's at Disney's Grand Floridian Resort & Spa.

2¾ cups whole wheat flour

1½ teaspoons coarse salt

1 cup warm water (105°F to 115°F)

1 teaspoon granulated sugar

One ¼-ounce package active dry yeast

2 tablespoons olive oil

1 tablespoon flax seeds

¼ teaspoon freshly ground pepper for sprinkling

1. Into a medium bowl, sift together the flour and 1 teaspoon of the salt.

2. In a small bowl, combine ¼ cup of the water, the sugar, and the yeast. Let the mixture stand for about 5 minutes, or until foamy.

3. Add the yeast mixture to the flour mixture with the remaining ¾ cup water and 1 tablespoon plus 1 teaspoon of the olive oil. Mix with a wooden spoon to form a soft dough.

4. On a lightly floured surface, knead the dough for 7 to 8 minutes, or until smooth and elastic.

5. Place the dough in a lightly oiled bowl, cover the bowl with plastic wrap, and set aside to rise in a warm place for 45 minutes to 1 hour, or until doubled in size.

6. Preheat the oven to 500°F. On a lightly floured surface, punch down the dough, add the flax seeds, and knead briefly.

7. Roll out the dough to a 12-inch by 15-inch by ¼-inch-thick rectangle. Brush with the remaining 2 teaspoons olive oil and sprinkle with the remaining ½ teaspoon salt and the pepper. ☞

8. Transfer the dough to a baking sheet and bake, preferably on a pizza stone, for about 6 minutes.

Disney Institute Tip: You may use this recipe to bake pizza at home. Spread or sprinkle your favorite topping over the shaped dough and bake on a pizza stone in the 500°F oven for about 6 minutes.

Seven-Grain Bread

Chef Erich Herbitschek,
Disney's Grand Floridian
Resort & Spa Bakery

Makes 1 loaf.

Any combination of steel-cut grains works in this recipe.

1¼ cups warm water (105°F to 115°F)

½ cup steel-cut seven-grain cereal

2 tablespoons vegetable oil

Two ¼-ounce packages active dry yeast

1 teaspoon granulated sugar

2 cups all-purpose flour, or as needed

½ cup dark rye flour

2 teaspoons salt

1. In a medium bowl, combine ¾ cup of the warm water with the seven-grain cereal and the vegetable oil. Set aside for 20 minutes.

2. In a large bowl, combine the remaining ½ cup water with the yeast and the sugar and let stand for 5 minutes, or until foamy.

3. Add the seven-grain cereal mixture to the yeast mixture with 2 cups all-purpose flour, the rye flour, and the salt. Stir until thoroughly combined. On a lightly floured surface, knead the dough for 8 to 10 minutes, or until smooth and elastic; add up to ¼ cup of flour if the dough is too sticky.

4. Transfer the dough to a lightly oiled bowl, cover with a towel, and set aside to rise in a warm place 1½ to 2 hours, or until doubled in size. ☞

5. On a lightly floured surface, punch down the dough and shape it into a round loaf about 6 inches in diameter. Place the loaf seam-side down on a lightly oiled baking sheet, cover with a towel, and set aside to rise in a warm place 1 to 1½ hours, or until doubled in size.

6. Preheat the oven to 400°F.

7. Bake for 30 to 35 minutes, or until the loaf is golden brown and sounds hollow when tapped on the bottom.

Disney Institute Tip: If you have a seven-grain cereal on hand made with rolled grains rather than steel-cut grains, feel free to use it for this recipe. Proceed as directed, but leave out the grain soaking step.

Pine Nut Bread

Chef Scott Hunnel,
Victoria & Albert's

Makes 1 loaf.

Follow the tradition set by Disney's award-winning Victoria & Albert's and serve this dense, sweet bread with fresh fruit, an assortment of imported cheeses, and Port.

½ cup pine nuts

½ cup milk

3 tablespoons butter, at room temperature

3 tablespoons solid vegetable shortening, at room temperature

¾ cup granulated sugar

1 cup bread flour

1 cup pastry flour

2 teaspoons baking soda

½ teaspoon salt

2 large eggs, lightly beaten

1. Preheat the oven to 325°F. Lightly grease an 8½-inch by 4½-inch loaf pan.

2. In a small bowl, soak the pine nuts in the milk.

3. In a medium bowl, with an electric mixer, beat the butter, shortening, and sugar together until light and creamy.

4. Into a medium bowl, sift together the bread flour, pastry flour, baking soda, and salt.

5. Add the dry ingredients to the butter mixture, alternating with the eggs, and beat until smooth. Add the pine nuts with the milk and stir until thoroughly blended.

6. Pour the batter into the prepared pan. Bake for 55 to 60 minutes, or until the loaf is golden brown. Cool on a rack before serving.

Blueberry Corn Bread

Chef Lenny DeGeorge,
Cinderella's Royal Table

Makes 3 mini loaves.

At Cinderella's Royal Table in the Magic Kingdom, Chef Lenny DeGeorge serves this tasty corn bread with barbecued chicken—a perfect combination.

6   tablespoons butter, at room temperature

2   large eggs

2   cups all-purpose flour

1   cup yellow cornmeal

¼   cup granulated sugar

2½   teaspoons baking powder

½   cup milk

½   cup orange juice

1   teaspoon finely grated orange zest

1   cup fresh blueberries, picked over

1. Preheat the oven to 375°F. Lightly grease three 3-inch by 5-inch mini loaf pans.

2. In a large bowl, with an electric mixer, beat the butter until smooth. Add the eggs and beat until thick and creamy.

3. Into a bowl, sift together the flour, cornmeal, sugar, and baking powder.

4. Alternately add the flour mixture, milk, orange juice, and zest to the butter mixture, beating well after each addition. The batter will be very stiff. With a rubber spatula, fold in the blueberries.

5. Using about 1¼ cups of the batter per loaf, spoon the batter into the prepared pans.

6. Bake the loaves for about 25 minutes, or until a wooden pick inserted in the center comes out clean. Cool on a rack before serving. ☛

7. To serve the bread as it's done at Cinderella's Royal Table, cut each loaf in half diagonally and in a heavy medium-size skillet, heat a bit of butter. Add the bread with the cut sides down and cook until it's browned, crispy, and heated through.

Penny's Poppyseed Muffins

Chef Penny Stone,
Disney's Yacht & Beach
Club Resort Bakery

Makes 6 muffins.

Here's the perfect muffin for a light breakfast or to enjoy with a steaming cup of afternoon tea.

1 cup plus 2 tablespoons cake flour

¼ cup granulated sugar

1 tablespoon baking powder

½ teaspoon salt

½ cup milk

3 tablespoons butter or margarine, melted and cooled

1 large egg

2 teaspoons finely grated lemon zest

2 teaspoons poppyseeds

1 teaspoon pure vanilla extract

1. Preheat the oven to 400°F. Lightly grease six 3-inch muffin cups.

2. Into a large mixing bowl, sift together the cake flour, sugar, baking powder, and salt. Make a well in the center.

3. In a medium bowl, whisk together the milk, melted butter, egg, lemon zest, poppyseeds, and vanilla.

4. With a fork, gently stir the milk mixture into the dry ingredients and mix just until combined; do not overmix.

5. Spoon the batter into the prepared muffin cups, filling them about ¾ full.

6. Bake for 5 minutes, reduce the heat to 350°F, and bake for 10 minutes longer, or until golden brown.

Pizza Crust

Chef Brad Gilliland,
Pizzafari

Makes crust for three 12-inch pizzas or 4 calzones.

Brush the pizza dough with olive oil and top with fresh herbs, cheese, vegetables, or whatever your heart desires. Caramelized onions, olives, and fresh rosemary would be terrific. Use this crust to make Vegetable Calzones too (recipe, page 63).

1 ¼ cups warm water (105°F to 115°F)

1 teaspoon granulated sugar

One ¼-ounce package active dry yeast

2 tablespoons olive oil

3 cups all-purpose flour, or as needed

1 teaspoon salt

1. In the bowl of an electric mixer, stir together the water and the sugar and sprinkle with the yeast. Set aside for 5 minutes, or until foamy. Add the olive oil.

2. Add 3 cups flour and the salt. With the dough hook, beat on high speed for 3 to 4 minutes, or until the mixture forms a smooth soft ball.

3. On a lightly floured surface, knead the dough for 4 to 5 minutes, or until smooth and elastic; add up to ¼ cup flour if the dough is too sticky.

4. Place the dough in a lightly oiled bowl, cover with a towel, and set aside to rise in a warm place for about 1 hour, or until doubled in size.

5. On a lightly floured surface, punch down the dough. Divide the dough into 3 equal pieces for three 12-inch pizzas or 4 equal pieces for the Vegetable Calzones.

6. For pizza, on a lightly floured surface, roll each piece of dough into a 12-inch circle. Top as desired and bake on a pizza stone in a 500°F oven for about 6 minutes, or until crust is crisp and browned.

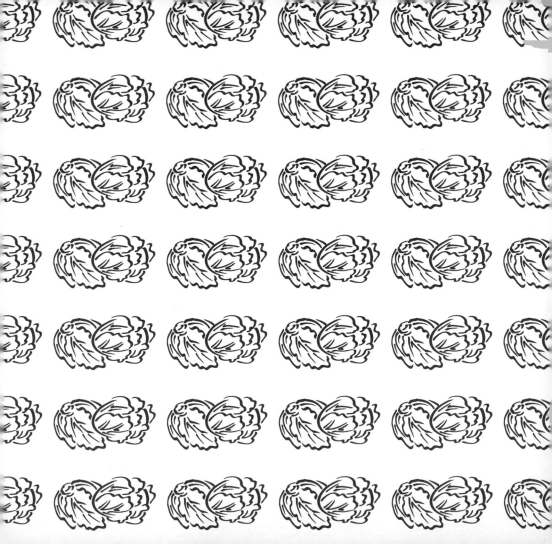

Hollywood Brown Derby Cobb Salad

Chef Michael LaDuke,
The Hollywood Brown Derby

Serves 4 to 6.

The grandmother of all great salads, this is the original, real, honest, and true Cobb Salad.

1 cup chopped iceberg lettuce leaves, washed and spun dry

1 cup chopped chicory leaves, washed and spun dry

1 cup tender sprigs watercress, washed and spun dry plus additional sprigs for garnish

1 pound poached turkey breast, finely chopped

2 medium-sized ripe tomatoes, peeled, seeded, and finely chopped

1 avocado, peeled, seeded, and finely chopped

½ cup crumbled blue cheese (about 2½ ounces)

6 strips bacon, cooked crisp, drained, and crumbled

3 hard-cooked eggs, peeled and finely chopped

2 tablespoons snipped fresh chives

½ cup Hollywood Brown Derby Old-Fashioned French Dressing (recipe follows)

Radicchio cups for serving

1. Toss the iceberg lettuce, chicory, and watercress together and arrange in a salad bowl.

2. In straight and separate lines, arrange the turkey, tomatoes, avocado, blue cheese, bacon, and eggs on top of the greens.

3. Sprinkle the chives in two diagonal lines across the salad.

4. To serve, present the salad at the table, toss with the dressing, and place in radicchio cups on chilled plates with watercress sprigs as garnish.

Disney Institute Tip: Depending on the size of your head of radicchio, and how many people you're planning to serve, you will need 8 to 12 radicchio leaves to make the cups for serving the salad.

Hollywood Brown Derby Old-Fashioned French Dressing

Makes about ½ cup.

2 tablespoons water

2 tablespoons red wine vinegar

1 tablespoon fresh lemon juice

½ teaspoon Worcestershire sauce

½ teaspoon salt, or to taste

½ teaspoon minced garlic

¼ teaspoon sugar

⅛ teaspoon freshly ground pepper, or to taste

⅛ teaspoon dry English mustard

⅓ cup vegetable oil

2 tablespoons olive oil

1. In a small bowl, whisk together the water, red wine vinegar, lemon juice, Worcestershire sauce, salt, garlic, sugar, freshly ground pepper, and dry mustard until well blended.

2. Whisking constantly, add the vegetable oil and the olive oil in a slow steady stream until the dressing is emulsified.

3. Store covered and chilled until ready to serve. Whisk the dressing to blend just before serving.

Beet and Arugula Salad

Chef Bart Hosmer,
Spoodles

Serves 4.

The more different types of beets you use for this salad, the more gorgeous it will be. Chiogga beets, also known as candy cane beets, have concentric circles of red and white and are quite stunning.

4 cups arugula leaves, washed and spun dry

Orange Vinaigrette (recipe, page 140)

12 slices peeled cooked beets, preferably red beets, Chiogga beets, and golden beets

½ cup toasted walnut halves

½ cup Parmesan cheese shaved with a vegetable peeler

1. In a bowl, toss the arugula with about ¼ cup of the Orange Vinaigrette until well coated. Giving it height, arrange the arugula on 4 salad plates.

2. In the same bowl, toss the beets with the remaining ¼ cup Orange Vinaigrette until well coated. Arrange the beets around the arugula.

3. Garnish the salad with the walnuts and the Parmesan cheese and serve immediately.

Braised Red Cabbage

Chef Craig Babbony,
Biergarten Restaurant

Serves 4; makes about 3 cups.

Part of the traditional German fare on the bountiful buffet at the Biergarten Restaurant in Epcot, this simple dish goes best with hearty meats and roast chicken.

1 **large head red cabbage (about 2 pounds), shredded**

1 **cup distilled white vinegar**

1 **cup granulated sugar**

1 **teaspoon salt, or to taste**

1 **teaspoon caraway seed**

   A pinch ground cloves

1. In a 4- to 5-quart Dutch oven, bring the cabbage, distilled white vinegar, granulated sugar, salt, caraway seed, and ground cloves to a boil over medium-high heat.

2. Reduce the heat to low, cover, and simmer, stirring occasionally, for 35 to 40 minutes, or until the cabbage is very tender and most of the liquid has evaporated.

Carrots and Cranberries

Chef Jeff Page,
Crystal Palace

Serves 6 to 8; makes about 4 cups.

This is a terrific dish to serve for Thanksgiving dinner. You can make it ahead—prepare the components separately and heat them together just before you're ready to serve.

1⅓ cups orange juice

3 tablespoons light brown sugar

1 tablespoon cornstarch

2 tablespoons butter

2 pounds carrots, peeled and thinly sliced

1 cup fresh cranberries

½ teaspoon salt, or to taste

⅛ teaspoon freshly ground pepper, or to taste

1. In a 1-quart saucepan, bring 1 cup of the orange juice and the brown sugar to a simmer over medium heat, stirring until the sugar is dissolved.

2. In a small bowl, whisk together the remaining ⅓ cup orange juice with the cornstarch. Add the cornstarch mixture to the brown sugar mixture and bring to a boil, whisking constantly, and cook for 1 minute, or until thickened. Set aside.

3. In a 12-inch skillet, melt the butter over medium heat. Add the carrots and cook, stirring, about 5 minutes, or until crisp-tender. Add the cranberries, salt, and pepper and cook, stirring, for 2 minutes longer. Add the thickened orange juice mixture, combine thoroughly, and cook about 2 minutes, or just until heated through.

4. Transfer to a serving bowl and serve hot.

Cabernet Whipped Potatoes

Chef Hans Rouillard,
Epcot Catering

Serves 4; makes about 3½ cups.

Simple whipped potatoes get a lift from Cabernet.

1½ cups Cabernet Sauvignon wine

1 cup finely chopped shallots

4 bay leaves

10 whole black peppercorns

2 pounds russet potatoes, peeled and cut into ½-inch pieces

¼ cup (½ stick) butter, melted

1 teaspoon salt, or to taste

½ teaspoon freshly ground pepper, or to taste

1. In a 2-quart saucepan, bring the Cabernet Sauvignon wine, shallots, bay leaves, and peppercorns to a boil over high heat, and boil until the liquid is reduced by half.

2. Meanwhile, in a 3-quart saucepan, bring the potatoes and enough salted cold water to cover to a low boil over medium heat, and cook until very tender, about 15 minutes. Drain the water from the pan, shake the pan over high heat for 30 seconds, or until any excess liquid is evaporated, and remove from heat.

3. Puree the potatoes through a food mill while still hot. Strain the reduced red wine into the potatoes (discard the solids), add the melted butter, and whisk until smooth and light. Season with salt and pepper.

Roasted Garlic and Grilled Eggplant Whipped Potatoes

Chef Hans Rouillard,
Epcot Catering

Serves 4; makes about 4 cups.

Start with ordinary mashed potatoes, then add an abundance of garlic and eggplant to create a whole new sensation—you may never make regular mashed potatoes again.

1 **small eggplant (about 12 ounces), trimmed, peeled, and cut crosswise into ½-inch slices**

Olive oil for brushing

2 **pounds russet potatoes, peeled and cut into ½-inch pieces**

1 **whole head Roasted Garlic (recipe page 164)**

½ **cup milk, heated**

¼ **cup (½ stick) butter, melted**

1 **teaspoon salt, or to taste**

½ **teaspoon freshly ground pepper, or to taste**

1. Prepare charcoal for grilling or heat a gas grill. On a work surface, brush one side of each eggplant slice with olive oil. Grill the eggplant, oiled side down, on a lightly oiled rack set over glowing coals for 6 to 8 minutes, or until softened and browned. Brush the top side with oil, turn, and grill for 6 to 8 minutes longer, or until cooked through.

2. In a 3-quart saucepan, bring the potatoes and enough salted cold water to cover to a low boil over medium heat, and cook until very tender, about 15 minutes. Drain the water from the pan, shake the pan over high heat for 30 seconds, or until any excess liquid is evaporated, and then remove from heat.

3. Puree the potatoes, eggplant, and the roasted garlic through a food mill, while the potatoes are still hot. Add the heated milk and melted butter, and whisk until smooth and light. Season with salt and pepper to taste.

Anna Potatoes

Chef Russell Klein,
Concourse Steakhouse

Serves 6.

This easy-to-assemble "potato pie" would complement many meat or fish entrées, and makes an unusually pretty presentation.

2½ pounds Idaho baking potatoes (4 or 5 large potatoes)

Vegetable oil cooking spray

½ cup freshly grated Parmesan cheese

6 tablespoons butter, cut into small pieces

½ cup finely chopped shallots

¼ cup snipped fresh chives

2 teaspoons minced garlic

¾ teaspoon salt, or to taste

¼ teaspoon coarsely cracked black peppercorns, or to taste

1. Preheat the oven to 400°F. Place a 12-inch cast iron skillet over medium-low heat.

2. Peel the potatoes and slice lengthwise as thin as possible; ¹⁄₁₆-inch is ideal.

3. Spray the bottom and the sides of the hot skillet with the vegetable oil cooking spray. Cover the bottom and the sides with 1 layer of potatoes.

4. Sprinkle the potatoes with 1 layer of Parmesan cheese, butter, shallots, chives, garlic, salt, and pepper. Cover with another layer of the potatoes, leaving no gaps. Add another layer of cheese, butter, and seasonings. Follow this with a layer of potatoes, then cheese, butter and seasonings, and finally potatoes.

5. Spray the top layer with vegetable oil cooking spray. Bake for 40 to 50 minutes, or until the top is browned and crisp.

6. Remove the skillet from the oven and let the potatoes stand for 10 minutes. Carefully invert the potato cake onto a large serving plate. Slice and serve immediately, or let cool and then reheat just before serving.

Vegetable Calzone

Chef Brad Gilliland,
Pizzafari

Serves 8.

Loaded with vegetables and cheese, this version of a calzone is a big hit with hungry guests at Disney's Animal Kingdom.

Pizza Crust dough (recipe page 52)

2 tablespoons olive oil

1 cup chopped onion

1 cup finely chopped broccoli florets

½ cup finely chopped carrots

½ cup finely chopped celery

1 teaspoon minced garlic

¾ cup favorite store-bought pizza sauce

½ teaspoon salt, or to taste

¼ teaspoon freshly ground pepper, or to taste

⅔ cup coarsely grated cheddar cheese

⅔ cup coarsely grated Gruyère cheese

⅔ cup coarsely grated fontina cheese

½ cup ricotta cheese

½ cup oil-packed sun-dried tomatoes, drained and chopped

1 large egg, lightly beaten

1. Divide pizza crust dough into 4 equal pieces. On a lightly floured surface, roll out each piece into a 9-inch circle.

2. Preheat the oven to 375°F.

3. In a 10- or 12-inch skillet, heat the olive oil over medium heat until hot but not smoking. Add the onion and cook, stirring, for 5 minutes, or until softened. Stir in the broccoli, carrots, celery, and garlic and cook, stirring, for 5 minutes, or until softened. Stir in the pizza sauce, salt, and pepper. Remove the skillet from the heat.

4. In a bowl, stir together the cheddar, Gruyère, fontina, and ricotta cheeses and the dried tomatoes. ☞

5. Evenly divide the vegetable mixture over the 4 dough circles and spread over half of each circle to within ¾ inch of the edge. Top with the cheese mixture. Moisten the edge of the dough with water, fold the dough in half over the filling, and seal the edge by pressing together with the tines of a fork. With a fork, prick the tops and brush the tops with the lightly beaten egg.

6. Lightly oil 2 large baking sheets and place 2 calzones on each. Bake for 30 to 35 minutes, or until the crust is lightly browned.

7. Cut each calzone in half and serve hot.

Grilled Eggplant Sandwich

Chef Darryl Mickler,
Disney-MGM Studios
Catering

Serves 6.

The fabulous array of flavors in this sandwich is well worth the time needed to prepare it.

⅔ **cup olive oil**

3 **tablespoons fresh lemon juice**

1 **garlic clove, minced**

1 **large eggplant, peeled and cut crosswise into twelve ½-inch-thick slices**

12 **large slices hearty bread**

Yogurt and Boursin Spread (recipe, page 19)

Twelve ½-inch-thick red onion slices

12 **thin slices fontina cheese**

Red Pepper Sauce (recipe page 18)

3 **cups assorted baby greens**

1. In a 9-inch by 13-inch glass baking dish, combine ⅓ cup of the olive oil, 2 tablespoons lemon juice, and garlic. Add the eggplant and marinate, turning occasionally, 1 to 2 hours.

2. Prepare charcoal for grilling or heat a gas grill. Measure out 3 tablespoons of the olive oil and, dividing it equally, brush some onto one side of each bread slice. Grill the bread over glowing coals until lightly browned, about 1 minute per side. Spread the oiled side of each bread slice with the Yogurt and Boursin Spread.

3. Grill the eggplant slices and the onion slices for 5 minutes, or just until edges begin to brown. Turn the eggplant and the onions over, top the eggplant with the cheese, and grill about 6 minutes, or until the eggplant and the onion are tender and the cheese is melted. Stack the onion slices on top of the cheese and eggplant.

4. Arrange the eggplant stacks on 6 bread slices and top with the Red Pepper Sauce. ☞

5. Toss the baby greens with the remaining olive oil and lemon juice and place on Red Pepper Sauce. Top with remaining 6 bread slices and make 6 sandwiches, pressing bread slices together gently. Serve immediately.

Disney Institute Tip: If you're pressed for time, skip marinating the eggplant and brush it with the olive oil and lemon juice while it's on the grill. Prepare the sandwich on a stove-top ridged grill pan when outdoor grilling isn't convenient. You can also make the Red Pepper Sauce and the Yogurt and Boursin Spread a day ahead.

Fish and Shellfish

Spice-Crusted Tuna

Chef John State,
Flying Fish Café

Serves 4.

This quick and easy way to prepare fresh tuna is one of the most requested recipes at the Flying Fish Café at Disney's BoardWalk.

1 tablespoon crushed fennel seeds

1 tablespoon crushed coriander seeds

1½ teaspoons coarse salt

1 teaspoon coarsely cracked black peppercorns

Four 1-inch-thick tuna steaks (about 6 ounces each)

3 tablespoons olive oil

1. On a dinner plate, mix together the fennel seeds, coriander seeds, salt, and peppercorns.

2. Press the tuna steaks into the spice mixture to evenly coat all sides.

3. In a 12-inch skillet, heat the olive oil over high heat until hot but not smoking. Add the tuna steaks and, turning with tongs, sear all sides, about 7 to 8 minutes, or until browned and crusty for rare, or longer for desired doneness.

4. To serve, slice the tuna steaks in half lengthwise and serve cut side up.

Disney Institute Tip: A quick and easy way to crush fennel seeds, coriander seeds, and black peppercorns is to place them in a resealable plastic bag, seal the bag tightly, and on a work surface, hit the spices with a small, heavy, flat-bottomed saucepan or skillet. They'll be nicely crushed without scattering all over your kitchen.

Cedar Plank Salmon

Chef Robert Adams,
Artist Point

Serves 4.

For striking flavor, this salmon is set on a plank of red cedar and oven-roasted. A 10-inch by 10-inch plank should be large enough for most filets.

- 1 **red cedar plank**
- 2 **tablespoons walnut oil**
- 2 **tablespoons pure maple syrup**
- 2 **tablespoons bourbon whiskey**
- One **16-ounce salmon filet, preferably wild king salmon**
- 6 **fresh rosemary sprigs**
- 6 **fresh thyme sprigs**

1. Preheat the oven to 400°F.

2. Heat the red cedar plank in the oven for 15 minutes. Brush the plank with the walnut oil. In a small bowl, whisk together the maple syrup and the bourbon whiskey.

3. Place the salmon on the cedar plank, arrange the rosemary and thyme sprigs on top, and drizzle with the maple syrup and bourbon whiskey mixture.

4. Roast the salmon for 20 to 25 minutes, or until just opaque throughout.

The Wine Steward Suggests: Cedar Plank Salmon will taste great with a Pinot Noir or a medium-bodied Chardonnay. The soft tannins, firm structure, and ripe fruit of a Pinot Noir enhance the texture of the fish and complement the woody flavors in this recipe. If you prefer a white wine, a Chardonnay made in the Burgundian style will offer viscosity and richness and will be in harmony with the palate.

Roasted Mahi Mahi

Chef Michael Schifano,
Olivia's Cafe

Serves 4.

An abundance of fresh vegetables accompanies this oven-roasted fish. Serve it with snappy Sun-Dried Tomato and Caper Vinaigrette (recipe, page 139).

4 tablespoons olive oil

Four 8-ounce mahi mahi filets

1 teaspoon coarse salt, or to taste

¼ teaspoon freshly ground pepper, or to taste

1½ cups finely chopped sweet onion

1 cup sliced mushrooms

2 plum tomatoes, seeded and thinly sliced lengthwise

2 cups baby spinach leaves, washed and spun dry

4 cups finely shredded kale, washed and spun dry

½ cup Sun-Dried Tomato and Caper Vinaigrette (recipe, page 139)

1. Preheat the oven to 375°F. Oil a 9-inch by 13-inch baking pan with 1 tablespoon of the olive oil.

2. Season each mahi mahi filet on both sides with salt and pepper and place in the baking pan. Top with 1 cup of the sweet onion, cover the pan tightly with aluminum foil, and bake for 13 minutes. Remove the foil and cook the fish and the onion for 2 to 3 minutes more, or until the fish is just opaque throughout and the onion is softened.

3. Meanwhile, in a 10- to 12-inch skillet, heat 1 tablespoon of the olive oil over medium-high heat until hot but not smoking. Add the mushrooms and cook, stirring, for 4 minutes, or until lightly browned. Add the remaining ½ cup sweet onion and cook, stirring, for 1 minute. Add the tomatoes, season with salt and pepper, and cook, stirring, for 1 minute, or until the tomatoes are tender. Transfer the mixture to a bowl and stir in the spinach. ☞

4. In the same skillet, heat the remaining 2 tablespoons olive oil. Add the kale and cook, stirring, for 1 to 2 minutes, or until wilted. Remove the skillet from the heat, add the Sun-Dried Tomato and Caper Vinaigrette, and stir to blend. Add the kale to the mushroom mixture and season with salt and pepper.

5. To serve, arrange warm vegetables on 4 serving plates and top with roasted mahi mahi.

The Wine Steward Suggests: Because mahi mahi has a subtle flavor, any seasoning used to cook it becomes dominant. Complement this vibrant recipe with a fruity, refreshing wine such as Viognier.

Tomato-Basil Poached Sea Bass

Chef Christine Weissman,
Seasons

Serves 8.

Spa guests at the Disney Institute often request this light, healthful entrée.

4 cups fish stock or clam broth or clam broth and water

Eight 5-ounce pieces sea bass

40 stalks pencil-thin asparagus, trimmed and cooked crisp-tender

16 fingerling potatoes or tiny red potatoes, sliced on the diagonal and cooked

4 cups Clear Tomato Broth (recipe, page 165)

3 tablespoons Spiced Basil Oil (recipe, page 165)

24 fresh basil leaves, washed and spun dry

1 medium-sized ripe tomato, peeled, seeded, and cut into 1-inch diamonds

1. In a 12-inch skillet, heat the fish stock to a simmer over medium heat. Add the sea bass and gently poach for 4 to 5 minutes, or just until opaque throughout; insert a sharp knife or a skewer into the fish to check for doneness, if necessary. With a slotted spoon, transfer the fish to a plate and keep warm.

2. In a 10-inch skillet, heat the Clear Tomato Broth over medium-high heat until very hot. Add the cooked asparagus and the potatoes and cook, stirring frequently, for about 4 minutes, or until the asparagus and the potatoes are heated through.

3. Using a slotted spoon, evenly divide the asparagus and the potatoes among 8 shallow serving bowls. Top each serving with a piece of the sea bass. Spoon the Clear Tomato Broth over the fish and the vegetables, using about ½ cup per serving. ☞

4. Garnish each serving with 3 fresh basil leaves and a few tomato diamonds. Then drizzle each with a generous teaspoon of the Spiced Basil Oil. Serve hot.

Disney Institute Tip: If you prefer, use your favorite bottled or fresh vegetable juice (dilute it a bit if you'd like) instead of the Clear Tomato Broth. But do make the Spiced Basil Oil—it's terrific to have in your refrigerator for quickly flavoring pasta, fish, and poultry dishes.

John's Crab Cakes

Chef John State,
Flying Fish Café

Makes 28 small crab cakes.

These smaller size crab cakes are perfect for nibbling before a meal. If you'd rather serve them as the main course, just make the crab cakes larger. You'll be able to serve 4 to 6.

6 cups soft fresh bread crumbs

1 pound lump crabmeat, picked over

½ cup finely chopped red onion

½ cup each finely chopped red and green bell pepper

½ cup finely chopped scallions

½ cup mayonnaise

1 poblano chile, trimmed, seeded, and minced

4 large egg yolks

2 tablespoons fresh lemon juice

1 tablespoon chopped fresh parsley

1¾ teaspoons salt, or to taste

1¼ teaspoons freshly ground pepper, or to taste

⅛ teaspoon cayenne pepper, or to taste

1 cup all-purpose flour

5 large eggs

½ cup vegetable oil for frying

Chile Rémoulade (recipe, page 131)

1. In a large bowl, stir together 2 cups of the bread crumbs, the crabmeat, red onions, red and green bell pepper, scallions, mayonnaise, poblano chile, egg yolks, lemon juice, parsley, ¾ teaspoon salt, ¼ teaspoon freshly ground pepper, and the cayenne pepper.

2. Form 28 crab cakes, using about 2 tablespoons crab mixture for each and shaping to about 1½ inches in diameter.

3. On a plate, stir together the flour and the remaining 1 teaspoon salt and 1 teaspoon pepper. In a shallow bowl, with a fork, lightly beat the eggs. Place the remaining bread crumbs on a plate. ☞

4. Dip each crab cake into the flour, shaking off the excess, then into egg, shaking off the excess, and finally into the bread crumbs, shaking off the excess. Place the crab cakes on a baking rack.

5. In a 12-inch skillet, heat ¼ cup of the vegetable oil over medium-high heat until hot but not smoking. Add the crab cakes, in batches, and cook for 3 to 4 minutes on each side, or until browned and crisp. As the crab cakes are cooked, remove them with a slotted spoon and drain on paper towels; keep warm. Repeat to cook the remaining crab cakes, adding more oil as necessary. Serve hot with the Chile Rémoulade.

The Wine Steward Suggests: John's Crab Cakes call for some spice in the wine. Try a Gewürztraminer, which offers flowery fragrances with a touch of spiciness. The acidity is well balanced and reciprocates food flavors.

BBQ Shrimp Orleans

Chef Paul Nichols,
Bonfamille's Café

Serves 4.

Close your eyes and you're in New Orleans! All this intense, fabulous flavor makes a lovely entrée for a dinner party. Or, you could serve the shrimp as an appetizer—just omit the garlic bread and the rice.

- **1 pound medium shrimp**
- **1 tablespoon plus 1 teaspoon Cajun seasoning**
- **1 teaspoon coarsely cracked black peppercorns, or to taste**
- **2 tablespoons olive oil**
- **½ cup chopped onion**
- **2 garlic cloves, minced**
- **2 cups water**
- **2 tablespoons fresh lemon juice**
- **1 teaspoon Worcestershire sauce**
- **¼ cup dry white wine**
- **1 teaspoon salt, or to taste**
- **1 bay leaf**
- **2 cups heavy cream**

  Hot cooked white rice for serving
- **2 tablespoons butter, at room temperature**

  Garlic bread for serving
- **¼ cup chopped fresh parsley for garnish**

1. Peel and devein the shrimp, leaving the tails on. Reserve the shrimp shells for the sauce.

2. In a small bowl, mix together 1 tablespoon of the Cajun seasoning with ½ teaspoon of the cracked black peppercorns. Rub the mixture into the shrimp. Store the shrimp, covered and chilled, until ready to use.

3. In a 2- to 3-quart saucepan, heat 1 tablespoon of the olive oil over medium-high heat until hot but not smoking. Add the onion and garlic and cook, stirring, for 1 minute.

4. Add the shrimp shells, water, lemon juice, Worcestershire sauce, dry white wine, remaining 1 teaspoon Cajun seasoning, salt, remaining ½ teaspoon cracked black peppercorns, and bay leaf. Bring the mixture to a boil, reduce the heat to low, and simmer for 15 minutes. ☛

5. Remove the pan from the heat and allow the mixture to cool. Strain the liquid into a small saucepan, discarding the solids. Bring the liquid to a boil over high heat and cook for about 15 minutes, or until the liquid is reduced to ¼ cup and is thick, syrupy, and brown.

6. In a 12-inch skillet, heat the remaining 1 tablespoon olive oil over high heat until hot but not smoking. Add the shrimp and cook, stirring, for 2 minutes. Add the cream and the sauce mixture and simmer, stirring, for 3 to 5 minutes.

7. Arrange the rice on 4 warm serving plates. With a slotted spoon, remove the shrimp and place on the rice.

8. Whisk the butter into the sauce, remove the skillet from the heat, and ladle the sauce over the shrimp and on the front of the plates. Arrange the garlic bread on the side and garnish the plates with the chopped parsley. Serve hot.

Disney Institute Tip: There are lots of Cajun seasonings on the market. Try a few to see which you like best.

Meat and Poultry

Mom's Meatloaf

Chef Marianne Hunnel,
50's Prime Time Cafe

Serves 8.

Since not all of us have moms who make terrific meatloaf, here's a recipe that can take the place of a passed-along favorite. The leftovers make great sandwiches.

2 pounds ground beef

1 pound ground pork

4 large eggs, lightly beaten

1 cup seasoned bread crumbs

½ cup finely chopped onion

¼ cup finely chopped green bell pepper

¼ cup finely chopped red bell pepper

2 tablespoons plus ½ teaspoon Worcestershire sauce

½ teaspoon coarsely cracked black peppercorns, or to taste

½ teaspoon coarse salt, or to taste

½ cup ketchup

1 tablespoon brown sugar

1 teaspoon Dijon mustard

1. Preheat the oven to 350°F. Lightly oil two 8½-inch by 4½-inch loaf pans.

2. In a large bowl, combine the beef, pork, eggs, bread crumbs, onion, green bell pepper, red bell pepper, 2 tablespoons Worcestershire sauce, cracked peppercorns, and salt just until well blended; do not overmix.

3. Divide the meat mix in half, shape into 2 loaves, and place in the prepared loaf pans. Bake for 50 to 60 minutes, or until the internal temperature taken with an instant-read thermometer is 155°F.

4. Meanwhile, in a small bowl, stir together the ketchup, brown sugar, mustard, and the remaining ½ teaspoon Worcestershire sauce. Brush the meatloaf with the ketchup mixture and bake for 10 minutes longer.

5. Remove the meatloaf from the oven and let stand for 10 minutes before serving.

Grilled Pork Tenderloin

Chef Clifford Pleau,
California Grill

Serves 4.

To make this entrée less complicated, omit one of the accessory dishes. You could serve the pork tenderloin with just the polenta or just the mushroom glaze.

6 tablespoons olive oil

20 fresh sage leaves with stems

½ teaspoon salt, or to taste

¼ teaspoon freshly ground pepper, or to taste

1 pound pork tenderloin, trimmed

½ cup Mustard Butter (recipe, page 127)

Garlic and Herb Polenta (recipe, page 109)

1 cup Balsamic Mushroom Glaze (recipe, page 129)

1. In a 10-inch skillet, heat ¼ cup of the olive oil over medium-high heat until hot but not smoking. Add 5 of the sage leaves and turn quickly, cooking for only 10 seconds; immediately, with a slotted spoon, transfer the sage leaves to paper towels to drain. Repeat with the remaining sage leaves. Set aside at room temperature until ready to serve.

2. On a plate, stir together the remaining 2 tablespoons of the olive oil, the salt, and the pepper. Completely coat the pork tenderloin with the olive oil mixture.

3. Preheat an empty 10-inch cast iron skillet over medium-high heat until very hot. Add the pork and sear, turning with tongs to brown all sides. Reduce the heat to medium and cook, turning frequently and basting occasionally with the Mustard Butter, for about 15 minutes, or just until the pork is cooked through. Set the pork aside, covered, on a cutting board, for 5 minutes to let the juices settle. ☞

4. To serve, arrange the Garlic and Herb Polenta on 4 warm serving plates. Cut the pork loin crosswise into 20 thick slices and arrange 5 slices on each serving of polenta. Ladle the Balsamic Mushroom Glaze over the pork and top each serving with 5 leaves of fried sage.

The Wine Steward Suggests: The pork and polenta are best complemented by a big, satisfying, full red wine like a Châteauneuf-du-Pape. Its juicy, spicy, slightly dusty character goes well with such filling foods.

Beef Filet with Chipotle

Chef Roger Hill,
Yachtsman Steakhouse

Serves 4.

Chipotles are dried and smoked jalapeño peppers—sure to wake up your tastebuds.

2 **large chipotle peppers, soaked in warm water to cover for 20 minutes**

1 **roasted red bell pepper**

¼ **cup olive oil**

¼ **cup oil-packed sun-dried tomatoes, drained**

1 **tablespoon tequila**

2 **garlic cloves, minced**

1 **teaspoon chopped cilantro plus additional sprigs for garnish**

½ **teaspoon ground cumin seed**

Four 8-ounce filet mignons (each 1¼ to 1½ inches thick)

1 **teaspoon salt, or to taste**

¼ **teaspoon freshly ground pepper, or to taste**

Monterey Jack Cheese Grits (recipe, page 110)

¼ **cup Pumpkin Seed— Cilantro Butter (recipe, page 126)**

Sour cream for garnish

1. Drain, trim, and seed the chipotles, reserving the liquid. In a food processor, puree the chipotle with the roasted red pepper, olive oil, sun-dried tomatoes, tequila, garlic, chopped cilantro, and cumin until smooth.

2. Prepare charcoal for grilling or heat a gas grill (you can also use a broiler). Season the filets with salt and pepper. Grill the filets on a lightly oiled rack set over glowing coals, turning once, for 7 to 9 minutes for medium-rare, or to desired doneness. When cooked to desired doneness, remove filets from the grill and coat with the chipotle mixture. Return to the grill and quickly sear the filets, 1 minute per side. ☞

3. To serve, divide the Monterey Jack Cheese Grits among 4 serving plates. Place a filet on each serving and top with a tablespoon of the Pumpkin Seed–Cilantro Butter. Garnish each serving with fresh cilantro sprigs and a dollop of sour cream.

The Wine Steward Suggests: The Beef Filet with Chipotle is a hearty dish; balance it with a hearty wine such as Cabernet Sauvignon.

Krautwickel

Chef Craig Babbony,
Biergarten Restaurant

Serves 6.

These authentic cabbage rolls are always popular on the buffet in the Germany Pavilion at Epcot.

12 fresh cabbage leaves, washed and with stems removed

6 slices bacon, cut into ½-inch pieces

1 onion, finely chopped

10 ounces small white mushrooms, trimmed and sliced

½ cup dried porcini mushrooms, soaked in warm water for 20 minutes, drained, and chopped

2 medium-sized potatoes, boiled, peeled, and mashed

2 cups soft fresh bread crumbs

1 bunch chives, trimmed and snipped

½ teaspoon salt, or to taste

¼ teaspoon freshly ground pepper, or to taste

⅛ teaspoon freshly grated nutmeg

¼ cup heavy cream

2 large eggs, lightly beaten

2 cups chicken and/or beef broth

1. In a large pot of boiling salted water, blanch the cabbage leaves for 4 to 5 minutes, or just until softened. Drain in a colander and refresh with cold water to stop the cooking.

2. In a 10- to 12-inch skillet, cook the bacon, stirring, over medium heat, until crisp. With a slotted spoon, transfer the bacon to paper towels to drain.

3. Add the onion and fresh mushrooms to the skillet and cook, stirring, for 8 to 10 minutes, or until golden brown. Add the porcini mushrooms and cook, stirring, for 2 minutes longer.

4. Remove the skillet from the heat. Stir in the mashed potato, bread crumbs, reserved cooked bacon, snipped chives, salt, pepper, and nutmeg. ☞

5. Lightly whip the heavy cream and fold into the mushroom mixture with the lightly beaten eggs.

6. Preheat the oven to 350°F. On a work surface, lay out the cabbage leaves. Place about ½ cup stuffing in the middle of each cabbage leaf, fold the sides in over the filling, and roll up loosely. Secure each roll with a wooden pick.

7. Place the cabbage rolls in a 13-inch by 9-inch baking pan, add the broth, and cover tightly with aluminum foil. Bake for 30 to 35 minutes, or until cooked through.

Disney's Grand Floridian Mango Chicken

Chef Dan Kniola,
Grand Floridian Cafe

Serves 8.

Sweet mangoes are the perfect complement to baked chicken. At the Grand Floridian Cafe, this dish is served with shoestring fries and fresh vegetables.

1 cup orange juice

½ cup honey

½ cup frozen pineapple juice concentrate

2 tablespoons bottled Rose's lime juice

1 tablespoon coarsely cracked black peppercorns

2 teaspoons garlic powder

2 teaspoons salt

2 whole chickens, halved (about 3½ pounds each)

Disney's Grand Floridian Mango Sauce (recipe, page 128)

1. In a roasting pan just large enough to hold the chickens in a single layer, stir together the orange juice, honey, pineapple juice, Rose's lime juice, cracked black peppercorns, garlic powder, and salt. Add the chicken halves, turn to coat, and marinate, covered and chilled, turning occasionally, for 2 hours.

2. Preheat the oven to 350°F.

3. Drain the marinade from the chicken and bake, turning once, for 45 to 50 minutes, or until the juices run clear when the chicken is pierced with the tip of a paring knife.

4. Arrange the chicken halves on a large serving platter, spoon the Mango Sauce over the chicken, and serve hot.

The Wine Steward Suggests: Grand Floridian Mango Chicken and a red Zinfandel are an ideal combination, with the "jamminess" in the wine intensifying the fruit flavors and diminishing the acidity of the mango.

Chicken with Peach-Ginger Sauce

Chef Jeff Page,
Crystal Palace

Serves 4.

Prepare this dish in the midst of winter, and you just might feel that you're on summer vacation—it has great summertime flavor.

One 15-ounce can peaches packed in their own juice, drained and liquid reserved

1 **tablespoon cornstarch**

3 **tablespoons butter**

1 **shallot, minced**

2 **tablespoons thinly sliced peeled fresh ginger**

2 **tablespoons honey**

One 3- to 3½-pound whole chicken, cut into serving pieces

2 **tablespoons favorite seasoning salt (such as Lawry's)**

1. Preheat the oven to 375°F. Sprinkle the chicken with the seasoning salt. Place the chicken in a roasting pan and bake for 1 hour, or just until the chicken is cooked through.

2. Meanwhile, in a small bowl, using a fork, combine ¼ cup of the reserved peach juice with the cornstarch.

3. In a medium saucepan, melt 1 tablespoon of the butter over medium-low heat until the foam subsides. Add the shallot and the ginger and cook, stirring, until the shallot is translucent, about 2 minutes.

4. Add the peaches and the honey and cook over low heat, stirring, for 5 minutes, or until almost all of the liquid has evaporated. Increase the heat to medium-high, add the cornstarch mixture, bring to a boil, and boil for 1 minute, stirring constantly, until the sauce is thickened.

5. Whisk in the remaining 2 tablespoons butter until melted. In a food processor or blender, puree the sauce in batches and strain through a fine sieve, pressing hard on the solids. Keep the Peach-Ginger Sauce warm. ☛

6. To serve, arrange the chicken on four serving plates and top with the Peach-Ginger Sauce. Serve immediately.

Disney Institute Tip: Give this sauce a try on grilled or broiled chicken, roast duck, or grilled pork chops—all will be superb.

Banana Leaf Wrapped Chicken

Chef Michael George,
'Ohana

Serves 8 as an appetizer or 4 as a main course.

Mouth-watering aromas fill the air when you unwrap the green banana leaves right at the table. If you can't find banana leaves, parchment paper, available in most supermarkets, works just fine.

- ½ **cup soy sauce**
- ¼ **cup molasses**
- 2 **tablespoons chopped peeled fresh ginger**
- 2 **teaspoons minced garlic**
- ½ **teaspoon liquid smoke**
- ½ **teaspoon Worcestershire sauce**
- ⅛ **teaspoon freshly ground pepper, or to taste**
- 8 **skinless boneless chicken thighs (about 1½ pounds)**
- 8 **banana leaves or 8 pieces parchment paper, cut into 10-inch by 6-inch pieces**

1. In a medium bowl, combine the soy sauce, molasses, ginger, garlic, liquid smoke, Worcestershire sauce, and pepper and mix well. Place the chicken in a 1 gallon plastic freezer bag, add marinade to coat, and seal closed. Marinate, chilled, overnight.

2. Preheat the oven to 325°F.

3. On a work surface, lay out 1 banana leaf and place 1 chicken thigh in the center; fold in both ends of the banana leaf, and then fold in both sides. Place the chicken package seam side down in a roasting pan. Repeat, to wrap the remaining chicken thighs, and then cover the pan tightly with aluminum foil.

4. Bake the chicken for 40 minutes, or until cooked through.

5. To serve, arrange the chicken packages family style on a large platter and have the diners serve themselves and unwrap their own packages.

Chicken with Olives and Preserved Lemons

Chef Darryl Mickler,
Disney-MGM Studios
Catering

Serves 8.

Let this dish transport you to sunny Morocco. You don't need exotic ingredients, but you do have to plan ahead to prepare the preserved lemons.

½ cup chopped flat-leaf parsley

½ cup chopped cilantro

1 tablespoon minced garlic

1 tablespoon paprika

1 teaspoon ground ginger

1 teaspoon ground cumin

½ teaspoon salt, or to taste

¼ teaspoon freshly ground pepper, or to taste

A pinch saffron threads, crumbled

8 chicken quarters

4 medium onions, halved and very thinly sliced

2 tablespoons butter

8 preserved lemon quarters, rinsed (recipe page 164)

1¾ cups Mediterranean-style green olives, rinsed and pitted

1. In a large bowl, combine the parsley, cilantro, garlic, paprika, ginger, cumin, salt, pepper, and saffron. Add the chicken quarters and toss well to coat completely. Marinate, covered and chilled, for 1 to 4 hours.

2. In a 4- to 5-quart Dutch oven, arrange the chicken. Top with 2 cups water, the onions, and the butter. Over medium-high heat, bring the mixture to a boil, reduce the heat to medium-low, cover, and simmer gently, stirring occasionally, for 50 minutes. Add the preserved lemons and the olives and cook for another 15 minutes, or until the chicken is very tender and cooked through.

3. Transfer the chicken, olives, and preserved lemons to a serving platter; keep warm. Reduce the pan juices over high heat for about 15 minutes, or until the sauce is very thick. Spoon the sauce over the chicken and serve immediately.

Rice, Pasta and Grains

Coconut Ginger Rice

Chef Jeff Page,
Crystal Palace

Serves 6 to 8; makes about 6 cups.

Use this rice dish to turn a very simple entrée, like grilled or broiled chicken, into a very special meal—with the taste of the Caribbean.

2 tablespoons vegetable oil

¼ cup julienned peeled fresh ginger

2 cups long-grain white rice, rinsed and drained

4 cups water

½ cup well-stirred canned coconut milk

2 chopped scallions plus 2 thinly sliced scallions for garnish

1½ teaspoons salt, or to taste

¼ teaspoon cracked black peppercorns, or to taste

1. In a 10- to 12-inch skillet with a lid, heat the oil over medium heat until hot but not smoking. Add the ginger and cook, stirring, for 2 minutes, or until very fragrant. Add the rice, and cook, stirring, for 1 minute, or until it crackles.

2. Add the water, coconut milk, chopped scallions, salt, and cracked pepper and stir to blend. Reduce the heat to low, cover, and cook, for 20 to 25 minutes, or until the rice is cooked through.

3. Serve the rice hot, garnished with the 2 remaining thinly sliced scallions.

Lemongrass Risotto

Chef Clifford Pleau,
California Grill

Serves 4; makes about 4 cups.

An abundance of lemon gives this risotto a very refreshing flavor. Add some grilled or sautéed shrimp just before serving to turn it into a very satisfying main course.

About 5 cups vegetable stock

¼ cup olive oil

½ cup finely chopped onion

¼ cup finely chopped lemongrass (tender parts only)

2 tablespoons grated peeled fresh ginger

2 teaspoons minced garlic

2 cups Arborio rice

1 teaspoon salt, or to taste

¼ teaspoon freshly ground pepper, or to taste

2 teaspoons finely grated lemon zest

1. In a 2-quart saucepan, heat the vegetable stock to a boil, reduce the heat, and keep at a bare simmer.

2. In a 3- to 4-quart saucepan, heat the oil over medium heat. Add the onion, lemongrass, ginger, and garlic and cook, stirring, for 5 to 6 minutes, or until the onion and lemongrass are softened. Add the rice, and cook, stirring, for 5 minutes, or until the ends are translucent.

3. Add about ½ cup of the simmering stock to the rice, and cook, stirring constantly, until all the stock is absorbed. Continue cooking and adding stock, about ½ cup at a time, stirring constantly and letting each addition be absorbed before adding the next, until the rice is al dente, about 20 minutes; season with salt and pepper about halfway through the cooking time. When the rice is almost done, add the lemon zest, then taste and adjust the seasonings.

4. Place the risotto on 4 warm serving plates or shallow bowls and serve immediately.

Risotto with Lamb, Olives and Red Peppers

Chef Darryl Mickler,
Disney-MGM Studios
Catering

Serves 8 to 10 as an appetizer or 6 as a main course; makes about 9 cups.

This satisfying marriage of flavors has proved very popular at catered dinners at the Disney-MGM Studios.

- ¼ cup olive oil
- 1½ pounds lean leg of lamb, cut into 1-inch pieces
- 3 cups low-sodium beef broth
- 3 cups low-sodium chicken broth
- 6 shallots, finely chopped
- 2 garlic cloves, minced
- 1 teaspoon ground cumin seed
- 1½ cups **Arborio rice**
- ¾ cup dry white wine
- ½ teaspoon salt, or to taste
- ¼ teaspoon freshly ground pepper, or to taste
- 2 roasted red bell peppers, peeled, seeded, and chopped
- ½ cup pitted **Kalamata olives**
- ⅓ cup freshly grated **Parmesan cheese**
- ¼ cup finely chopped fresh parsley

1. In a 4- to 5-quart Dutch oven, heat 2 tablespoons of the olive oil over medium heat until hot but not smoking. Brown the lamb in two batches, 8 to 10 minutes each batch. With a slotted spoon, transfer the lamb to a plate, and set aside.

2. In a 3- to 4-quart saucepan, combine the beef broth and the chicken broth and bring to a simmer.

3. In the same 4- to 5-quart Dutch oven, heat the remaining 2 tablespoons olive oil over medium heat until hot but not smoking. Add the shallots, garlic, and cumin and cook, stirring, for 6 to 7 minutes, or until the shallots are translucent.

4. Stir in the rice and cook, stirring constantly, for 4 minutes. Stir in the wine and cook, stirring constantly, until the wine has evaporated. ☛

5. Add the lamb and just enough of the broth to cover the rice. Stir once and let cook until almost all the broth is absorbed, about 8 minutes. Season with salt and pepper.

6. Add the remaining broth ½ cup at a time, stirring and allowing the rice to cook until almost all the broth is absorbed before adding more; never allow the rice to dry out; it should take about 25 minutes.

7. When ready to serve, stir in the roasted red bell peppers, olives, Parmesan cheese, and parsley. Serve on warmed plates.

Disney Institute Tip: Arborio rice is a short-grain, high-starch pearl rice that, when cooked, releases its starch to make a very creamy dish.

The Wine Steward Suggests: Risotto with Lamb, Olives and Red Peppers is an elaborate dish calling for a special wine. Try a Barolo or Gattinara from Northwestern Italy; either will force your palate to distinguish the aromas and flavors.

Portobello Mushroom Pasta

Chef Marianne Hunnel,
50's Prime Time Café

Serves 2; makes about 2½ cups.

Portobello mushrooms are extremely large (up to 6 inches in diameter) and have a deep rich flavor and a great meaty texture. You'll find them either whole or sliced in most produce sections.

- **2** tablespoons olive oil
- **1** tablespoon balsamic vinegar
- **1** portobello mushroom cap, cut into 1-inch pieces
- **6** artichoke hearts, preferably fresh, but drained canned or thawed frozen are fine
- **½** cup chopped, peeled, and seeded ripe tomato
- **½** cup sugar snap peas
- **¼** cup dry white wine
- **1** teaspoon minced garlic
- **2** cups cooked bow tie pasta, rinsed in cold water and drained
- **2** tablespoons freshly grated Parmesan cheese
- **1** tablespoon slivered fresh basil leaves for garnish

1. In a medium bowl, stir together 1 tablespoon of the olive oil with the balsamic vinegar. Add the portobello mushroom pieces and marinate at room temperature for 1 hour, turning occasionally.

2. In a 10- to 12-inch skillet, heat the remaining 1 tablespoon olive oil over medium heat until hot but not smoking. Add the portobello mushroom with the marinade, the artichoke hearts, tomato, sugar snap peas, wine, and garlic. Cook, stirring, about 2 minutes, or until the wine is reduced by half.

3. Stir in the cooked and drained pasta and the Parmesan cheese and cook, stirring, just until heated through.

4. Serve the pasta hot, garnished with the slivered fresh basil.

Chicken Caesar Pasta

Chef Jeff Page,
Crystal Palace

Serves 6; makes about 12 cups.

Using your favorite store-bought Caesar salad dressing makes this a very easy dish to prepare—one that can be on the table in minutes.

- **1 pound penne pasta**
- **¼ cup (½ stick) butter**
- **4 large skinless boneless chicken breast halves (about 2 pounds), cut into 1-inch pieces**
- **¼ teaspoon salt, or to taste**
- **⅛ teaspoon freshly ground pepper, or to taste**
- **1 cup favorite homemade or store-bought Caesar salad dressing, or as needed**
- **6 cups roughly chopped romaine lettuce leaves**
- **3 tablespoons freshly grated Parmesan cheese, or to taste**
- **Coarsely cracked black peppercorns to taste**

1. In a large pot of boiling salted water, cook the pasta according to package directions, or until al dente. Drain well.

2. In a deep 10- to 12-inch skillet, heat the ¼ cup butter over medium-high heat. Add the chicken, salt, and freshly ground pepper and cook, stirring, 7 to 8 minutes, or until the chicken is just cooked through. Add the pasta to the skillet and stir to combine.

3. Remove the skillet from the heat, add the Caesar salad dressing and 3 cups of the romaine lettuce, and stir until well blended. Add more dressing, as needed, if the 1 cup has been absorbed.

4. To serve, arrange the pasta in individual serving bowls, garnish with the remaining 3 cups romaine, the Parmesan cheese, and the cracked black pepper. Serve hot.

Country Penne

Chef Dee Foundoukis,
Tony's Town Square
Restaurant

Serves 6; makes about 12 cups

For a lighter version of this penne, omit the Italian sausage. Swiss chard or mustard greens can substitute for the spinach.

1 **pound sweet Italian sausage**

1 **pound penne pasta**

2 **tablespoons olive oil**

2 **cups broccoli florets, blanched**

2 **teaspoons minced garlic**

One 15-ounce can canellini beans, rinsed and drained

One 10-ounce package frozen artichoke hearts, thawed and halved

¼ **cup Basil Pesto (recipe, page 132) or store-bought pesto**

½ **teaspoon salt, or to taste**

¼ **teaspoon freshly ground pepper, or to taste**

One 15-ounce can tomato sauce

2 **cups fresh spinach leaves, washed and spun dry**

¼ **cup freshly grated Asiago cheese or Parmesan cheese for garnish**

1. Remove the sausage from the casing. In a 10-inch skillet, cook the sausage, stirring, over medium heat, until no pinkness remains. With a slotted spoon, transfer the sausage to paper towels to drain.

2. In a large pot of boiling salted water, cook the pasta according to package directions, or until al dente. Drain completely.

3. Meanwhile, in a 4- to 5-quart Dutch oven, heat the oil over high heat until hot but not smoking. Add the sausage, broccoli, and garlic and cook, stirring, for 2 minutes. Add the beans, artichoke hearts, pesto, salt, and pepper and cook, stirring, for 2 minutes. Stir in the pasta, tomato sauce, and spinach and cook, stirring, for 2 minutes.

6. Serve the pasta hot, garnished with the Asiago cheese.

Pasta with Mushroom Ragout and Pesto

Chef Anette Grecchi,
Narcoossee's

Serves 4 to 6; makes about 10 cups.

This dish can be prepared in advance, then assembled just before serving. Your favorite fresh or store-bought vegetable juice can be substituted for the tomato broth.

1½ cups halved fresh cremini mushrooms

1½ cups torn fresh oyster mushrooms

1½ cups sliced portobello mushrooms

2 tablespoons olive oil

¼ teaspoon salt, or to taste

⅛ teaspoon freshly ground pepper, or to taste

1 pound orrecchiette pasta

½ cup dried porcini mushrooms, soaked in warm water for 20 minutes and drained

1 cup Clear Tomato Broth (recipe, page 165)

1 cup coarsely shredded Gruyère cheese

¼ cup Basil Pesto (recipe, page 132) or store-bought pesto

1. Preheat the oven to 450°F.

2. In a large bowl, stir together the fresh mushrooms, olive oil, salt, and pepper. On a large baking sheet, arrange the mushrooms in a single layer. Roast the mushrooms, turning once, for 10 to 12 minutes.

3. Meanwhile, in a large pot of boiling salted water, cook the pasta according to package directions, or until al dente. Drain completely.

4. Just before serving, in a 4- to 5-quart Dutch oven, heat the fresh and dried mushrooms with the Clear Tomato Broth over medium heat. Add the drained pasta and cook, stirring, for 1 minute. Remove the Dutch oven from the heat and stir in ½ cup of the Gruyère cheese and the pesto.

5. Serve the pasta hot, garnished with the remaining ½ cup Gruyère cheese.

Rigatoni with Tapenade and Goat Cheese

Chef Bart Hosmer,
Spoodles

Serves 6 as an appetizer or 4 as a main course; makes about 8 cups.

A favorite at Spoodles, goat cheese and black olives offer a robust, Mediterranean flavor.

- **1 pound rigatoni pasta**
- **6 tablespoons Sun-Dried Tomato and Kalamata Olive Tapenade (recipe follows)**
- **2 tablespoons olive oil**
- **½ teaspoon salt, or to taste**
- **⅛ teaspoon freshly ground pepper, or to taste**
- **4 ounces soft mild goat cheese (such as Montrachet), crumbled, for garnish**
- **2 tablespoons very finely shredded fresh basil leaves, for garnish**

1. In a large pot of boiling salted water, cook the pasta according to package directions, or until al dente. Drain completely.

2. In a large bowl, toss the pasta with the Sun-Dried Tomato and Kalamata Olive Tapenade, the olive oil, salt, and pepper.

3. Transfer the pasta to serving bowls and garnish with the crumbled goat cheese and the basil.

Sun-Dried Tomato and Kalamata Olive Tapenade

Chef Bart Hosmer,
Spoodles

Makes about ½ cup.

This tapenade makes a terrific, full-flavored pasta sauce, or you can serve it as an appetizer with croutons or warm pita triangles. It also works very well as a topping for grilled or broiled fish.

½ cup oil-packed sun-dried tomato halves, drained

½ cup pitted Kalamata olives

1 tablespoon olive oil

1 tablespoon minced garlic

2 tablespoons freshly grated Parmesan cheese

1 tablespoon tomato sauce

1 tablespoon chopped fresh flat-leaf parsley

1 tablespoon chopped fresh basil leaves

1. In a food processor, puree the sun-dried tomatoes, olives, olive oil, and garlic.

2. Transfer the mixture to a bowl and stir in the Parmesan cheese, tomato sauce, parsley, and basil.

Disney Institute Tip: Consider making this tapenade in a larger quantity. You'll find lots of uses for it, and it will last for a couple of weeks in your refrigerator.

Sonoma Goat Cheese Ravioli

Chef Clifford Pleau,
California Grill

Serves 4 to 6.

Serve these ravioli in a shallow bowl of warm Clear Tomato Broth (recipe, page 165). Or even easier, try topping them with chopped seeded ripe tomatoes.

- **1 pound soft mild goat cheese (such as Montrachet), crumbled**
- **5½ ounces aged goat cheese, crumbled**
- **½ cup seasoned bread crumbs**
- **2 tablespoons Basil Pesto (recipe, page 132) or store-bought pesto**
- **2 teaspoons extra-virgin olive oil**
- **2 teaspoons Roasted Garlic puree (recipe, page 164)**
- **½ teaspoon salt, or to taste**
- **⅛ teaspoon freshly ground pepper, or to taste**
- **16 egg roll wrappers**
- **1 large egg and 1 tablespoon water for egg wash**

1. In a large bowl, stir together the fresh goat cheese, aged goat cheese, bread crumbs, pesto, olive oil, garlic, salt, and pepper until well combined.

2. On a work surface, lay out 8 egg roll wrappers and brush each with the egg wash. With a sharp knife, mark each wrapper into 4 squares, taking care not to cut all of the way through. Place about 1 tablespoon of the goat cheese mixture in the center of each square. Cover with the 8 remaining egg roll wrappers and press the edges together. With a knife, cut each double wrapper with filling into 4 squares, to yield 32 squares of filled ravioli. Press the edges together. (If you are not using the ravioli immediately, sprinkle them lightly with cornmeal, and store refrigerated between layers of waxed paper.)

3. When ready to serve, cook the ravioli in a large pot of boiling salted water for 1 to 2 minutes. Drain completely.

Uncle Giovanni's Vegetable Pasta

Chef Marianne Hunnel,
50's Prime Time Café

Serves 6 to 8; makes about 12 cups.

Pesto lends a savory accent to this fresh vegetable pasta dish.

- 1 **pound penne pasta**
- ⅓ **cup olive oil**
- 1 **cup small broccoli florets**
- 1 **cup sliced mushrooms**
- 1 **cup julienned yellow squash**
- 1 **shallot, minced**
- ⅓ **cup dry white wine**
- 2 **ripe tomatoes, peeled, seeded, and chopped**
- ¼ **cup Basil Pesto (recipe, page 132) or store-bought**
- ¾ **teaspoon salt, or to taste**
- ¼ **teaspoon coarsely cracked black peppercorns, or to taste**
- ½ **cup freshly grated Parmesan cheese**

1. In a large pot of boiling salted water, cook the pasta according to package directions, or until al dente. Drain.

2. Meanwhile, in a deep 12-inch skillet, heat the olive oil over medium-high heat until hot but not smoking. Add the broccoli, mushrooms, squash, and shallots and cook, stirring, for 6 minutes or until the vegetables are softened.

3. Add the white wine and cook until the liquid is reduced by half. Stir in the tomatoes, pesto, salt, and pepper and cook, stirring, for 1 minute. Add the pasta and cook, stirring, for 2 minutes, or until heated through.

4. To serve, transfer the pasta to serving plates and sprinkle with Parmesan cheese. Serve immediately.

Disney Institute Tip: To julienne the squash, cut it first into ¼-inch-thick slices, then into ¼-inch strips.

Spelt Tabbouleh

Chef Anette Grecchi,
Narcoossee's

Serves 4; makes about 4 cups.

Spelt, a centuries-old grain, is found in many health-food stores. Tart lemon and the crunchy grain create a terrific combination of texture and taste.

- 2 tablespoons extra-virgin olive oil
- ½ cup finely chopped onion
- 1 cup spelt berries or whole wheat berries
- 4 cups water
- 1 cup chopped flat-leaf parsley
- 2 large ripe tomatoes, peeled, seeded, and chopped
- 2 tablespoons fresh lemon juice, or to taste
- 1½ teaspoons finely grated lemon zest
- ¾ teaspoon coarse salt, or to taste
- ¼ teaspoon freshly ground pepper, or to taste

1. In a 4- to 5-quart Dutch oven, heat 1 tablespoon of the olive oil over medium heat until hot but not smoking. Add the onion and cook, stirring, for 5 to 6 minutes, or until the onion is softened.

2. Add the spelt berries and cook, stirring, for 3 minutes. Add the water and bring the mixture to a boil. Reduce the heat to low and simmer 35 to 40 minutes, or until the spelt is al dente and the water is absorbed. Transfer the spelt to a bowl and let cool to room temperature.

3. Meanwhile, in a large bowl, stir together the parsley, tomatoes, lemon juice, zest, salt, and pepper. Add the cooled spelt and stir to blend.

4. Just before serving, drizzle the salad with the remaining 1 tablespoon of the olive oil. Serve at room temperature.

Spiced Couscous

Chef Bart Hosmer,
Spoodles

Serves 4 to 6; makes about 5 cups.

Wonderful as a side dish for a summertime picnic, this recipe is sure to become a hot-weather favorite.

- **2 tablespoons olive oil**
- **½ cup chopped onion**
- **½ cup chopped fennel bulb**
- **2 carrots, peeled and finely chopped**
- **½ teaspoon salt, or to taste**
- **¼ teaspoon freshly ground pepper, or to taste**
- **2 cups chicken broth**
- **A pinch crushed hot red pepper flakes**
- **One 10-ounce package couscous (about 1¾ cups)**
- **¼ cup raisins**
- **2 tablespoons snipped fresh chives**

1. In a 10- to 12-inch skillet, heat the olive oil over medium heat until hot but not smoking. Add the onion, fennel, and carrots and cook, stirring occasionally, for 6 minutes, or until the carrot begins to soften and the onion and fennel are browned. Season with salt and pepper, transfer to a large bowl, and let cool to room temperature.

2. In a 3-quart saucepan, bring the broth and the crushed hot red pepper flakes to a boil. Remove the saucepan from the heat, add the couscous, cover, and let stand for 5 minutes. Fluff the grains with a fork and let cool to room temperature.

3. When both mixtures are cool, combine them with the raisins and the chives, tossing lightly to mix thoroughly. Serve at room temperature.

Disney Institute Tip: Try using whole wheat couscous for an even more nutritious dish. It has a nutty flavor that you might like even better.

Garlic and Herb Polenta

Chef Clifford Pleau,
California Grill

Serves 4 to 6; makes about 3 cups.

Created to serve with the Grilled Pork Tenderloin (recipe, page 82), this flavored polenta makes an unusually satisfying side dish.

1 tablespoon olive oil

½ cup finely chopped onion

2 teaspoons Roasted Garlic puree (recipe, page 164)

1¼ cups water

1¼ cups milk

⅓ cup heavy cream

½ cup yellow cornmeal

½ teaspoon salt, or to taste

⅛ teaspoon freshly ground pepper, or to taste

2 tablespoons grated Asiago or Parmesan cheese

¼ cup crumbled soft mild goat cheese (such as Montrachet)

1 tablespoon minced fresh thyme leaves

1 tablespoon minced fresh sage leaves

1 tablespoon chopped flat-leaf parsley for garnish

1. In a 3-quart saucepan, heat the olive oil over medium heat until hot but not smoking. Add the onions and cook, stirring, for 3 minutes, or until softened. Stir in the Roasted Garlic puree. Add the water, milk, and heavy cream and bring the mixture to a simmer over high heat.

2. Add the cornmeal in a slow steady stream, whisking constantly. Stir in the salt and pepper. Cook, stirring constantly, 15 to 20 minutes, or until thick and bubbling. Remove the saucepan from the heat and stir in the Asiago, goat cheese, thyme, and sage.

3. Serve the polenta hot, garnished with the parsley.

Monterey Jack Cheese Grits

Chef Roger Hill,
Yachtsman Steakhouse

Serves 4 to 6.

Forget potatoes or rice. These grits are the perfect accompaniment for beef. Serve them, for instance, with the Beef Filet with Chipotle (recipe, page 84).

2 tablespoons butter

¼ cup finely chopped onion

¼ cup finely chopped scallions

2 garlic cloves, minced

1½ cups chicken broth

1½ cups water

¾ cup quick-cooking grits

¼ cup heavy cream

1 teaspoon salt, or to taste

¼ teaspoon freshly ground pepper, or to taste

½ cup coarsely grated Monterey Jack cheese

1. In a 3-quart saucepan, heat 1 tablespoon of the butter over medium heat. Add the onion and scallions and cook, stirring, about 5 minutes, or until the onion is translucent. Add the garlic and cook, stirring, for 1 minute.

2. Add the broth and the water and bring the mixture to a boil over high heat. Add the grits in a slow steady stream, whisking constantly. Reduce the heat to low and simmer, stirring, for about 10 minutes, or until the grits are done.

3. Stir in the cream and season with the salt and the pepper. Remove the pan from the heat and whisk in the cheese and the remaining 1 tablespoon butter.

4. Serve hot. '

Children's
Favorites

Mémère's French Toast

Chef Paul Nichols,
Bonfamille's Cafe

Serves 4 to 6.

Much better than regular ol' French toast, this version has a delicious crackly crust of cinnamon sugar.

- **4** **large eggs**
- **½** **cup milk**
- **¾** **cup plus 2 tablespoons granulated sugar**
- **2½** **teaspoons ground cinnamon**
- **½** **teaspoon pure vanilla extract**
- **¼** **cup vegetable oil**
- **Twelve 1-inch thick bread slices (a 1-pound loaf)**
- **Warm maple or fruit syrup for serving**
- **Fresh fruit for serving (optional)**

1. In a medium bowl, whisk together the eggs, milk, 2 tablespoons sugar, ½ teaspoon cinnamon, and vanilla.

2. In a small bowl, stir together remaining ¾ cup sugar and 2 teaspoons ground cinnamon. Transfer the mixture to a plate and set aside.

3. In a 12-inch skillet, heat 1 tablespoon oil over medium heat. Three slices at a time, dip the bread into the egg mixture, and fry until golden brown on both sides.

4. Immediately dredge the hot cooked French toasts in the cinnamon sugar mixture and shake off excess.

5. Repeat with remaining slices and oil. Serve hot with warm maple or fruit syrup and fresh fruit, if desired.

Mickey Mouse Pancakes

Chef David Hutnick,
Chef Mickey's

Serves 4; makes 8 pancakes.

Make your weekend mornings more fun for you and your kids— serve Mickey-shaped pancakes. They're much easier to make than they look and may be the easiest way ever to get the kids to eat fresh fruit!

2 cups all-purpose flour

3 tablespoons sugar

2 teaspoons baking powder

¼ teaspoon salt

1½ cups milk

2 large eggs

2 tablespoons canola oil

½ teaspoon pure vanilla extract

Warm maple or fruit syrup for serving

Fresh fruit for serving

1. Into a large bowl, sift together the flour, sugar, baking powder, and salt; make a well in the center.

2. In a medium bowl, whisk together the milk, eggs, oil, and vanilla. Pour the milk mixture into the dry ingredients and stir just to blend.

3. Heat a lightly oiled griddle or a large skillet over medium heat until hot but not smoking. Using ¼-cup batter, make a 4-inch circle for the head. Using 2 tablespoons batter for each, make two 2-inch circles touching the top of the head for ears. When all the bubbles on the top of the pancake have popped and the underside is golden brown, use a pancake turner to flip all three circles as one pancake. Repeat with remaining batter.

4. Serve the pancakes hot with warm maple or fruit syrup and the fresh fruit of your choice.

Chef Mickey's Breakfast Pizza

Chef David Hutnick,
Chef Mickey's

Serves 6.

A great way to get your favorite children to eat breakfast, this dish also makes a lovely Sunday supper for the whole family.

One 12-inch Boboli pizza or other precooked pizza shell

½ cup coarsely grated mozzarella

½ cup coarsely grated provolone cheese

1 cup coarsely grated cheddar cheese

2 large eggs

¼ cup heavy cream

½ teaspoon salt, or to taste

A pinch fresh ground pepper, or to taste

1. Preheat the oven to 375°F. Place the pizza crust on a baking sheet.

2. In a medium bowl, blend the mozzarella, provolone, and cheddar cheeses.

3. In a small bowl, with a fork, beat together the eggs and the heavy cream and season with the salt and the pepper. Add to the cheese mixture.

4. Immediately, to avoid clumping, transfer the cheese mixture to the pizza shell.

5. Bake for 10 to 12 minutes, or until the cheese mixture is set and is beginning to brown.

6. Serve hot, cut into wedges.

Macaroni and Cheese

Chef David Hutnick,
Chef Mickey's

Serves 2 to 4; makes about 4 cups.

What child doesn't love old-fashioned comfort food? This classic staple with a dash of Worcestershire sauce disappears very quickly from the buffet at Chef Mickey's.

1 tablespoon butter
1 tablespoon all-purpose flour
½ cup milk
½ cup heavy cream
1 cup coarsely grated cheddar cheese
½ teaspoon Worcestershire sauce
¼ teaspoon salt, or to taste
⅛ teaspoon freshly ground pepper, or to taste
½ pound elbow macaroni, cooked and drained

1. In a 2-quart saucepan, heat the butter over medium heat. Add the flour and cook, stirring, for 2 minutes.

2. Remove the saucepan from the heat and slowly add the milk and heavy cream, stirring constantly, until well combined. Return the saucepan to the heat and cook, stirring, until the sauce is thickened. Remove the saucepan from the heat and add the cheese, stirring until smooth.

3. Stir in the Worcestershire sauce, salt, and pepper. Add the cooked and drained macaroni and stir until blended. Serve immediately.

Disney Institute Tip: Although this recipe calls for cheddar cheese, you may use the cheese you prefer.

Kid's Sushi

Chef Clifford Pleau,
California Grill

Makes 32 pieces.

Here's a terrific treat for kids that older children can make for themselves, once you show them how. A Kids' Sushi-making party would be great fun.

8 favorite flavor roll-up fruit snacks

3 tablespoons butter

3 cups mini-marshmallows

3 cups Rice Krispies

16 gummy worms

1. On a work surface, unroll the fruit snacks and lay them flat, with the plastic sheet down.

2. In a 3-quart saucepan, melt the butter over low heat. With a wooden spoon, stir in the marshmallows and continue cooking and stirring until the marshmallows are melted.

3. Stir the Rice Krispies into the melted marshmallow mixture.

4. Working quickly, with damp hands, spread about ½ cup of the Rice Krispies mixture over each fruit snack all the way to the bottom and sides, leaving a 1-inch space along the top. Arrange 2 gummy worms side by side at the bottom edge of the Rice Krispies mixture. Roll up tightly, jelly-roll fashion, peeling off the plastic sheet as you roll. Seal the roll with the 1-inch border at the top. Cut each roll crosswise into 4 even pieces.

Worms and Dirt

Chef Ed LaTour,
Garden Grill Restaurant

Serves 4.

The name makes grown-ups squirm, but kids love this clever, easy-to-make dessert.

2 cups milk

One 3.9-ounce package instant chocolate pudding mix

¾ cup Oreo cookie crumbs

8 gummy worms

1. In a mixing bowl, whisk together the milk and the chocolate pudding mix according to package directions.

2. With a spoon, place ¼ cup chocolate pudding in 4 small mason jars, glasses, or custard cups. Top each with 2 tablespoons Oreo cookie crumbs. Using about ¼ cup each serving, top with the remaining pudding to within ½ inch of the jar rim.

3. Finish with light dusting of Oreo cookie crumbs and place two gummy worms inside the jar, hanging over the rim.

4. Serve immediately, or chill, covered, and serve cold.

Children's Dessert Pizza

Chef Brad Gilliland,
Pizzafari

Serves 10 to 12.

Kids of all ages can't resist a slice of this rich and gooey dessert.

- **1 cup all-purpose flour**
- **½ cup graham cracker crumbs**
- **¼ cup granulated sugar**
- **¼ cup (½ stick) melted butter**
- **2¾ cups milk**
- **¼ cup cornstarch**
- **1 teaspoon pure vanilla extract**
- **2¼ cups semisweet chocolate chips**
- **3 cups mini-marshmallows**
- **1 cup heavy cream, beaten just to stiff peaks**

1. Preheat the oven to 400°F. Lightly oil a 10-inch pizza pan.

2. In a large bowl, stir together the flour, graham cracker crumbs, and 1 tablespoon of the sugar. Stir in the melted butter and ¼ cup of the milk; the mixture will be crumbly. Press the dough into the prepared pizza pan. Bake the crust for about 5 minutes, or until golden brown.

3. In a small bowl, mix together the cornstarch and the remaining 3 tablespoons sugar. Add ½ cup of the milk and stir to a smooth paste. In a 2-quart saucepan, heat the remaining 2 cups milk and bring just to a boil. Pour half of the milk into the bowl of cornstarch mixture and whisk until smooth. Return the cornstarch mixture to the saucepan and bring to a boil. Reduce the heat to low and cook, stirring, for 2 to 3 minutes, or until thickened and smooth. Remove the saucepan from the heat and stir in the vanilla. Let the custard cool to room temperature. ☞

4. In a 2-quart saucepan over very low heat, melt 2 cups of the chocolate chips, stirring, until smooth. Spread the cooled custard over the crust. Carefully spread the melted chocolate over the custard and top with the marshmallows. Bake the pizza for 3 to 4 minutes, or until the marshmallows are puffed and golden brown. Let the pizza cool for 15 to 20 minutes. Top with the whipped cream and the remaining ¼ cup chocolate chips.

5. Serve immediately, cut into slices.

Sauces

Flame Tree BBQ Sauce

Chef Hal Taylor,
Flame Tree Barbecue

Makes about 1½ cups.

This all-American BBQ sauce is especially good on pork and chicken.

- **1 cup ketchup**
- **¼ cup rice wine vinegar**
- **¼ cup water**
- **¼ cup packed light brown sugar**
- **2 tablespoons molasses**
- **1 tablespoon Worcestershire sauce**
- **1 tablespoon mild chili powder**
- **1 tablespoon paprika**
- **2 teaspoons onion powder**
- **1 teaspoon ground turmeric**
- **1 teaspoon ground cumin seed**
- **½ teaspoon garlic powder**
- **½ teaspoon ground cloves**

1. In a 2-quart saucepan, combine the ketchup, rice wine vinegar, water, brown sugar, molasses, Worcestershire sauce, chili powder, paprika, onion powder, ground turmeric, ground cumin, garlic powder, and ground cloves.

2. Bring the mixture to a simmer over medium heat, reduce the heat to low, and cook at a bare simmer, stirring frequently, for 35 minutes, or until thickened.

3. Use immediately or store, covered and chilled, for up to 2 weeks.

Hibiscus Honey Mustard Glaze

Chef Michael Bersell,
Captain's Tavern

Makes about 1 cup.

Chef Bersell uses this sweet glaze to finish the grilled mahi mahi at his restaurant at Disney's Caribbean Beach Resort.

2 tablespoons dried hibiscus flowers

½ cup warm water

½ cup Dijon mustard

½ cup honey

1. In a bowl, steep the hibiscus flowers in the warm water for 20 minutes. Drain completely, pat the flowers dry, and finely chop.

2. In a bowl, whisk together the chopped hibiscus flowers, Dijon mustard, and honey until well combined.

3. Use immediately or store, covered and chilled, for up to 2 weeks.

Disney Institute Tip: Apply the glaze to fish or chicken during the last few minutes of cooking (it's especially good on grilled foods) or thin the glaze with a little apple juice and use as salad dressing.

Disney Institute Tip: Hibiscus flowers are also called sorrel and are often available in Latino and Caribbean markets.

Sun-Dried Cherry Glaze

Chef Michael LaDuke,
The Hollywood Brown Derby

Serves 4 to 6; makes about 1½ cups.

Chef LaDuke finishes grilled filet mignon with this tart glaze, which complements almost any cut of beef.

1 cup Cabernet Sauvignon wine

1 cup sun-dried tart cherries

1 sprig fresh thyme

1 tablespoon sugar

1 cup low-sodium chicken and/or beef broth

2 tablespoons water

1 tablespoon cornstarch

¼ teaspoon salt, or to taste

⅛ teaspoon freshly ground pepper, or to taste

1. In a 2-quart saucepan, combine the Cabernet Sauvignon, ¾ cup sun-dried tart cherries, the fresh thyme, and the sugar over high heat. Bring the mixture to a boil and boil for 3 to 4 minutes, or until the volume of the liquid is reduced by half. Strain the mixture, return the liquid to the cleaned saucepan and discard the solids.

2. Add the broth and bring the mixture to a simmer.

3. In a small bowl, with a fork, combine the water with the cornstarch.

4. Add the cornstarch mixture to the broth mixture, bring to a boil, and boil, stirring constantly, for 1 minute, or until the sauce is thickened. Season with salt and pepper.

5. Stir in the remaining ¼ cup cherries and cook the mixture for 1 minute longer.

6. Use immediately or store, covered and chilled, for up to 1 week; gently reheat before using.

Pumpkin Seed— Cilantro Butter

Chef Roger Hill,
Yachtsman Steakhouse

Makes about ½ cup.

A dollop of this flavored butter is the perfect finish for the Monterey Jack Cheese Grits (recipe, page 110). Garnish with sprigs of fresh cilantro and a spoonful of sour cream. You can also use the butter to top baked or boiled potatoes.

¼ cup pumpkin seeds

6 tablespoons (¾ stick) butter, softened

2 teaspoons fresh lime juice

1 teaspoon fresh chopped cilantro

1 garlic clove, minced

1. In an 8-inch dry skillet, toast the pumpkin seeds, turning frequently, over medium-high heat, about 3 to 4 minutes. Transfer to a small bowl and let cool. With a food processor or a sharp knife, finely chop the pumpkin seeds.

2. In the same small bowl, stir together the pumpkin seeds, butter, lime juice, cilantro, and garlic and blend well.

3. Use immediately or store, covered and chilled, for up to 3 days.

Mustard Butter

Chef Clifford Pleau,
California Grill

Makes about ½ cup.

California Grill uses mustard butter to baste Grilled Pork Tenderloin (recipe, page 82). The butter also lends a distinctive flavor to grilled or baked chicken. The butter may be stored in the refrigerator for up to two weeks, or frozen for even longer.

6 tablespoons butter, softened

2 tablespoons Dijon mustard, at room temperature

2 tablespoons whole grain mustard (such as Pommery), at room temperature

2 teaspoons fresh lemon juice

1 teaspoon Worcestershire sauce

⅛ teaspoon freshly ground pepper, or to taste

1. In a small bowl, with a fork, combine all ingredients.
2. Transfer the Mustard Butter to a small bowl and store, covered and chilled, for up to 2 weeks.

Disney Institute Tip: To use this seasoned butter as a sauce for grilled meats, fish, or poultry, roll it into a log in a sheet of wax paper, freeze it, and then cut into thin slices to top the hot, grilled food—you'll have an instant sauce.

Disney's Grand Floridian Mango Sauce

Chef Dan Kniola,
Grand Floridian Cafe

Makes about 2 cups.

If you could bottle the sweetness of summer, this sauce would be it. Created at the Grand Floridian Café for its baked chicken (recipe, page 88), it's equally delicious on grilled or broiled fish.

2 cups chopped fresh ripe mango

1 roasted red bell pepper, peeled, seeded, and chopped

¾ cup ketchup

½ cup light brown sugar

½ cup chopped onion

¼ cup chopped dates

1 tablespoon Dijon mustard

1 teaspoon apple cider vinegar

1 teaspoon molasses

½ teaspoon minced garlic

¼ teaspoon ground cinnamon

¼ teaspoon ground cumin seed

1½ cups water

1. In a food processor, process the mango, roasted pepper, ketchup, brown sugar, onion, dates, Dijon mustard, apple cider vinegar, molasses, minced garlic, ground cinnamon, and ground cumin; mixture will not be smooth.

2. Transfer the mixture to a 2-quart saucepan and stir in the water. Bring the mixture to a boil, reduce the heat to low, and simmer gently for 30 minutes, or until thickened.

3. Use immediately or store, covered and chilled, for up to 1 week.

Balsamic Mushroom Glaze

Chef Clifford Pleau,
California Grill

Makes about 1 cup.

Zinfandel adds a subtle sweetness to this glaze. It's delicious in the Grilled Pork Tenderloin recipe on page 82, but you'll find it equally tasty on other meats or on poultry.

- ½ **pound cremini mushrooms**
- 1 **tablespoon olive oil**
- ½ **teaspoon coarse salt, or to taste**
- ⅛ **teaspoon freshly ground pepper, or to taste**
- 1 **cup Zinfandel Glaze (recipe, page 130)**
- 3 **tablespoons balsamic vinegar**

1. Preheat oven to 400°F.

2. In a medium bowl, toss the mushrooms with the olive oil, salt, and pepper. Spread the mushrooms in a single layer and roast, turning once, for 7 to 8 minutes, or until softened and browned.

3. In a 2-quart saucepan, bring the Zinfandel Glaze to a simmer over medium heat. Add the mushrooms and the balsamic vinegar and simmer for 10 minutes.

4. Strain the sauce through a fine sieve into a bowl. Brush onto meat or poultry while roasting or grilling. Store the sauce, covered and chilled, for up to 1 week.

Zinfandel Glaze

Chef Clifford Pleau,
California Grill

Makes about 1 cup.

A classic restaurant preparation, this reduction concentrates the flavors of wine, broth, mushrooms and herbs. Use it as the base for a sauce with very complex tastes, such as the Balsamic Mushroom Glaze on page 129.

1 **cup Zinfandel wine**

1 **red onion, finely chopped**

2 **cups chicken broth**

2 **cups finely chopped mushrooms**

2 **sprigs fresh thyme**

½ **teaspooon cracked whole black peppercorns**

¼ **cup meat trimmings**

3 **tablespoons all-purpose flour**

1. In a 2-quart saucepan, cook the wine and the onion over high heat for about 4 to 5 minutes, or until the liquid is reduced by half.

2. Add the broth, mushrooms, thyme, and peppercorns and reduce the liquid to about 1¼ cups.

3. Meanwhile, in a 10-inch skillet, brown the meat trimmings over medium heat. Add the flour and cook, stirring, for about 3 minutes, or until lightly browned.

4. Slowly whisk in the reduced wine mixture; cook, stirring, for 2 to 3 minutes, or until the mixture boils and thickens.

5. Strain the sauce through a fine sieve into a clean 1-quart saucepan; discard the solids. Use immediately or store, covered and chilled, for up to 1 week.

Chile Rémoulade

Chef John State,
Flying Fish Café

Makes about 2 cups.

Rémoulade is the classic topping for crab cakes, and this one, flavored with chile, is the best ever.

- **2 teaspoons chile powder, preferably ancho**
- **2 teaspoons water**
- **1½ cups mayonnaise**
- **¼ cup finely chopped red onion**
- **¼ cup finely chopped dill pickles**
- **2 tablespoons drained capers, chopped**
- **2 tablespoons finely chopped flat-leaf parsley**
- **2 tablespoons finely chopped fresh tarragon**
- **2 tablespoons snipped fresh chives**
- **2 tablespoons fresh lemon juice**
- **¼ teaspoon salt, or to taste**
- **¼ teaspoon cayenne pepper, or to taste**

1. In a small bowl, combine the chile powder with the water and let stand for 10 minutes.

2. In a mixing bowl, combine the chile mixture with the mayonnaise, red onion, dill pickles, capers, parsley, tarragon, chives, lemon juice, salt, and cayenne pepper.

3. Use immediately or store, covered and chilled, for up to 1 week.

Basil Pesto

Chef Anette Grecchi,
Narcoossee's

Makes about 1 cup.

This versatile and deliciously fragrant favorite complements pasta, poultry, vegetables, and even grilled fish.

2 cups loosely packed fresh basil leaves, washed and spun dry

4 large garlic cloves, crushed to a paste with a pinch of salt

½ cup extra-virgin olive oil

½ cup grated Asiago or Parmesan cheese

⅓ cup lightly toasted pine nuts

1 teaspoon coarse salt, or to taste

¼ teaspoon freshly ground pepper, or to taste

1. In a food processor, combine the basil and the garlic and pulse to puree. Through the feed tube, with the motor running, add the extra virgin olive oil in a slow steady stream and process to a fine, smooth puree.

2. Transfer the puree to a bowl, add the grated Asiago and the toasted pine nuts, and blend together.

3. Store covered and chilled. Serve at room temperature.

Disney Institute Tip: Pesto is best used within two days. However, if you'd like to make a big batch when fresh basil is abundant, prepare it through step 1 and freeze the mixture. Thaw before using and stir in the cheese, pine nuts, salt, and pepper.

Salad Dressings

Smokehouse Ranch Dressing

Chef Michael Deardorff,
Boatwright's Dining Hall

Makes about ¾ cup.

This dressing is terrific on green or vegetable salads. You can also use it as a dip for vegetables, chicken wings, or even chips!

- ⅓ **cup sour cream**
- ¼ **cup mayonnaise**
- 2 **tablespoons half-and-half**
- 1 **teaspoon minced garlic**
- 1 **teaspoon whole-grain mustard**
- ½ **teaspoon malt or apple cider vinegar**
- ½ **teaspoon salt, or to taste**
- ¼ **teaspoon dried tarragon leaves, crumbled**
- ¼ **teaspoon Tabasco sauce**
- ⅛ **teaspoon freshly ground pepper, or to taste**
- ⅛ **teaspoon Worcestershire sauce**
- ⅛ **teaspoon liquid smoke**
- ⅛ **teaspoon dried dill weed**
- **A pinch cayenne pepper, or to taste**

1. In medium bowl, whisk together all ingredients until well combined.
2. Chill, covered, until cold, about 30 minutes. Use immediately or store, covered and chilled, for up to 3 days.

Toasted Sesame Soy Sauce

Chef Michael George,
'Ohana

Makes ½ cup.

Diners request this salad dressing so often that the chef happily hands out copies of the recipe.

- **2** teaspoons vegetable oil
- **¼** cup finely chopped onion
- **¼** cup soy sauce
- **1** tablespoon plus 1½ teaspoons sweet rice wine
- **1** tablespoon plus 1½ teaspoons peanut butter
- **1** tablespoon sugar
- **1½** teaspoons toasted sesame seeds

1. In a small nonstick skillet, heat the oil over medium heat until hot but not smoking. Add the onion and cook, stirring frequently, for about 7 minutes, or until lightly browned.

2. Transfer the onion to a blender, add the soy sauce, sweet rice wine, peanut butter, sugar, and sesame seeds and blend until smooth. The sauce may thicken on standing; if desired, thin with water or broth.

3. Use immediately or store, covered and chilled, for up to 2 weeks.

Disney Institute Tip: Here's a salad dressing that can also be used as a robust marinade for meat or poultry. In fact, it makes a great sauce with anything grilled—especially vegetables.

Creole Herb Dressing

Chef Paul Nichols,
Bonfamille's Cafe

Makes 1⅔ cups.

A dressing with lots of Cajun flavor—consider giving this a try the next time you marinate chicken or pork.

- ½ cup mayonnaise
- ⅓ cup sour cream
- ¼ cup heavy cream
- ¼ cup milk
- ¼ cup chopped fresh parsley
- 1 tablespoon store-bought Cajun seasoning or blackened redfish seasoning
- ½ teaspoon granulated garlic
- ½ teaspoon Worcestershire sauce
- ½ teaspoon dried oregano, crumbled
- ½ teaspoon dried rosemary, crumbled
- ½ teaspoon dried thyme, crumbled
- ¼ teaspoon Tabasco sauce, or to taste
- ¼ teaspoon dried tarragon leaves, crumbled
- ½ teaspoon salt, or to taste
- ¼ teaspoon freshly ground pepper, or to taste
- A pinch cayenne pepper, or to taste

1. In a medium bowl, whisk together the mayonnaise, sour cream, heavy cream, milk, parsley, Cajun seasoning, granulated garlic, Worcestershire sauce, dried oregano, dried rosemary, dried thyme, Tabasco sauce, dried tarragon, salt, freshly ground pepper, and cayenne pepper.

2. Refrigerate, covered, overnight to allow flavors to develop. Store, covered and chilled, for up to 1 week.

Disney Institute Tip: Make this dressing as hot or as mild as you'd like by adjusting the amount of black pepper, cayenne pepper, and Tabasco sauce.

Raspberry Vinaigrette

Chef John Clark,
Coral Reef Restaurant

Makes about ¾ cup.

Tart yet sweet, this is the popular house dressing at Coral Reef Restaurant at Epcot.

½ pint raspberries

¾ cup raspberry vinegar

2 teaspoons sugar

1 teaspoon German-style mustard

½ teaspoon **Vinaigrette Spice (recipe, page 165)**

⅔ cup canola oil

1. Puree the raspberries in a blender or a food processor, and strain through a fine sieve into a small bowl, pressing hard on the solids; discard the solids.

2. To the raspberry puree, add the raspberry vinegar, sugar, mustard, and Vinaigrette Spice and whisk until blended.

3. Add the oil in a slow steady stream, whisking constantly until the dressing is emulsified. Use immediately or store, covered and chilled, for up to 3 days; whisk to combine just before using.

Sun-Dried Tomato and Caper Vinaigrette

Chef Michael Schifano,
Olivia's Cafe

Makes about ½ cup.

This simple but intensely flavored combination is warmed and tossed with vegetables for the Roasted Mahi Mahi (recipe, page 71). It's also great on a simple green salad.

- **2** tablespoons julienned sun-dried tomatoes
- **2** tablespoons minced red onion
- **2** tablespoons drained capers
- **2** tablespoons fresh lime juice
- **2** tablespoons champagne or white wine vinegar
- **1** teaspoon minced fresh basil leaves
- **1** teaspoon minced fresh thyme leaves
- **1** teaspoon minced fresh parsley
- **½** teaspoon salt, or to taste
- **⅛** teaspoon freshly ground pepper, or to taste
- **¼** cup olive oil

1. In a bowl, whisk together the sun-dried tomatoes, red onion, capers, lime juice, champagne vinegar, basil, thyme, parsley, salt, and pepper; let stand for 15 minutes.
2. Slowly add the olive oil, whisking constantly, until smooth. Use immediately or store, covered and chilled, for up to 2 weeks; whisk to combine just before using.

Orange Vinaigrette

Chef Bart Hosmer,
Spoodles

Makes about ½ cup.

A wonderful blend of citrus flavors, this dressing goes perfectly with the Beet and Arugula Salad (recipe, page 57).

¼ cup fresh orange juice

2 tablespoons fresh lemon juice

2 tablespoons chardonnay or other white wine vinegar

2 tablespoons honey

½ teaspoon ground coriander seed

½ teaspoon salt, or to taste

⅛ teaspoon freshly ground pepper, or to taste

A pinch cayenne pepper, or to taste

⅓ cup olive oil

1. In a 2-quart saucepan, reduce the volume of the orange juice and the lemon juice by half over high heat. Transfer the mixture to a bowl and whisk in the vinegar, honey, coriander, salt, freshly ground pepper, and cayenne pepper; let cool to room temperature.

2. Slowly add the olive oil, whisking constantly, until emulsified. Use immediately or store, covered and chilled, for up to 2 weeks; whisk to combine just before using.

Desserts and Pastries

Rice Cream with Strawberry Sauce

Chef John Morey,
Restaurant Akershus

Serves 4 to 6; makes about 5 cups rice pudding and 1 cup strawberry sauce.

This traditional Norwegian dessert is a delicious finish to the restaurant's *koldtbord*.

- 2 cups water
- ¼ teaspoon salt
- 1 cup short-grain white rice
- 2 cups milk
- 1 cup strawberry preserves
- 1 teaspoon fresh lemon juice
- 1 cup heavy cream
- ¼ cup sugar
- 1 teaspoon pure vanilla extract

1. In a 3- or 4-quart saucepan, bring 1½ cups of water to a boil with the salt. Add the rice, reduce the heat to medium-low, and cook the rice for 15 minutes, or until all of the water has been absorbed.

2. Add the milk and simmer for 20 minutes, or until all of the milk has been absorbed. Transfer the mixture to a bowl and let cool to room temperature.

3. Meanwhile, in a blender, combine the strawberry preserves, the remaining ½ cup water, and lemon juice and blend until smooth.

4. In a bowl, whip the cream with the sugar and vanilla. With a rubber spatula, fold the whipped cream mixture into the rice.

5. To serve, transfer the rice pudding to a large bowl or to individual serving bowls and drizzle with the strawberry sauce.

Cornmeal Cake with Fresh Fruit

Chef Andreas Born,
Disney's BoardWalk Bakery

Serves 8.

Try this dense, sweet cake to complement seasonal fruits.

- ¾ cup all-purpose flour
- ¼ cup yellow cornmeal
- 4 large eggs
- ¾ cup granulated sugar
- 1½ teaspoons finely grated lemon zest
- 1½ teaspoons finely grated orange zest
- 2 tablespoons orange juice
- 1½ teaspoons pure vanilla extract
- ¾ cup orange marmalade (or your favorite jam or preserves)
- Confectioners' sugar, for garnish
- 2 cups seasonal fresh fruit and berries for serving

1. Preheat the oven to 350°F. Grease and flour an 8-inch round cake pan and line the bottom with wax paper.

2. In a medium bowl, whisk together the flour and cornmeal.

3. In a large bowl, using an electric mixer, beat the egg yolks for 2 minutes, or until thick.

4. Slowly add ½ cup of the sugar and continue to beat 3 minutes, or until the egg yolks are thick and lemon-colored. Beat in the zests and the orange juice.

5. In a medium bowl, with clean beaters, beat the egg whites just to soft peaks. Slowly add the remaining ¼ cup sugar and the vanilla and continue to beat just to stiff peaks. With a rubber spatula, gently fold whites into yolk mixture. Sprinkle with the dry ingredients and fold in just until incorporated. ☞

6. Transfer the batter to the prepared cake pan and bake for 25 to 30 minutes, or until a wooden pick inserted in the center comes out clean. Cool the cake on a wire rack.

7. Remove the cake from the pan and, with a serrated knife, cut in half horizontally. Spread orange marmalade evenly over bottom layer and replace the top layer.

8. To serve, dust the cake with confectioners' sugar, cut into wedges, and serve with the fruit and berries.

Grapefruit Cake with Cream Cheese Frosting

Chef Michael LaDuke,
The Hollywood Brown
Derby

Serves 8.

This is the original
Grapefruit Cake, served
at the Hollywood Brown
Derby restaurant in the
1930s.

1 ½ cups sifted cake flour

¾ cup granulated sugar

1 ½ teaspoons baking powder

½ teaspoon salt

3 large eggs, separated

¼ cup vegetable oil

¼ cup water

3 tablespoons grapefruit juice

½ teaspoon finely grated lemon zest

¼ teaspoon cream of tartar

Grapefruit Cream Cheese Frosting (recipe follows)

One 16-ounce can grapefruit sections, drained well

1. Preheat the oven to 350°F. Lightly grease a 9-inch by 2-inch round cake pan. Line the bottom of the pan with wax paper and lightly grease the paper.

2. Into a large bowl, sift together the flour, sugar, baking powder and salt.

3. In a medium bowl, whisk together the egg yolks, oil, water, grapefruit juice, and lemon zest until smooth. Whisk in the flour mixture.

4. In a medium bowl, using an electric mixer, beat the egg whites and the cream of tartar just to stiff peaks. With a rubber spatula, gently fold the egg whites into the yolk mixture, until just blended. Pour into the prepared pan.

5. Bake for 25 to 30 minutes, or until the cake springs back when touched lightly in the center. Invert the cake, still in the pan, and cool on a wire rack. ☛

6. Run a spatula or a table knife around the edge of the cake. Carefully remove the cake from the pan. With a serrated knife, cut cake in half horizontally.

7. Spread the Grapefruit Cream Cheese Frosting on the bottom half of the cake. Top with several grapefruit sections. Cover with the second layer of the cake and frost the top and the sides.

8. Serve cake garnished with remaining grapefruit sections.

Grapefruit Cream Cheese Frosting

Makes about 2 cups.

Two 8-ounce packages cream cheese, softened

1 teaspoon fresh lemon juice

1 teaspoon finely grated lemon zest

1 cup sifted confectioners' sugar

6 drops yellow food coloring (optional)

1. In a medium bowl, using an electric mixer, beat the cream cheese on high speed until light and fluffy.

2. Add the lemon juice and the lemon zest. Gradually add the confectioners' sugar and beat until well blended. Add the food coloring, if desired.

Apple Strudel with Vanilla Sauce

Chef Craig Babbony,
Biergarten Restaurant

Serves 8.

Though it takes time and TLC, old-fashioned strudel is always a real crowd-pleaser.

1 cup all-purpose flour

½ cup bread flour

½ teaspoon salt

1 large egg yolk

¼ cup warm water

2 teaspoons vegetable oil plus additional for coating dough

¼ cup toasted bread crumbs

4 medium-sized Granny Smith apples, peeled, cored, and sliced

¼ cup raisins

¼ cup granulated sugar

¼ teaspoon ground cinnamon

¼ cup melted butter

Vanilla Sauce (recipe follows)

1. In the a bowl of an electric mixer, using the paddle on low speed, mix together the flours and the salt.

2. Slowly add the egg yolk, warm water, and 2 teaspoons of the oil. Put the mixer on medium speed and beat for 3 to 4 minutes, or until the dough pulls away from the side of the bowl and sticks slightly to the bottom of the bowl.

3. Remove the dough from the mixing bowl, lightly coat with oil, place in a self-sealing plastic bag (or a bowl covered with plastic wrap), and refrigerate overnight.

4. Preheat the oven to 400°F. Lightly oil a jelly roll pan.

5. Remove the dough from the refrigerator and gently wipe off any excess oil. For the best results, place the dough on a clean, lint-free towel on a work surface and gently pull the dough with your hands until it is paper-thin and rectangular in shape, about 16 inches by 14 inches. ☛

6. Place 3 tablespoons of the toasted bread crumbs on the long edge of the dough closest to you, forming a border approximately 3 inches wide.

7. In a large bowl, stir together the sliced apples and the raisins and arrange them on top of the toasted bread crumbs. In a small bowl, stir together the sugar and the cinnamon; sprinkle over the apples. Top the apples with the remaining 1 tablespoon toasted bread crumbs.

8. With a pastry brush, brush 2 tablespoons of the melted butter on the dough that is exposed. Next, grabbing the towel with the side where the apple mixture is, roll the dough to the other end, making certain that the apple mixture inside is even. Brush the outside of the dough with the remaining 2 tablespoons melted butter.

9. Transfer the strudel to the prepared pan and bake for 25 to 30 minutes, or until the strudel is golden brown. Let cool to room temperature.

10. To serve, cut with a serrated knife into 8 equal portions. Serve with Vanilla Sauce.

The Wine Steward Suggests: An *Eiswein* from Germany goes nicely with apple strudel.

Vanilla Sauce

Makes about 2 cups.

3 large egg yolks

⅓ cup granulated sugar

1 cup heavy cream

1 cup milk

1 teaspoon pure vanilla extract

1. In the bowl of an electric mixer, on medium speed, beat together the egg yolks and the sugar about 5 minutes, or until thick and lemon-colored.

2. In a medium saucepan, scald the heavy cream and the milk over medium heat. Remove the pan from the heat and allow to cool slightly.

3. With the mixer running on low speed, very gradually pour the scalded milk mixture into the egg yolk mixture. Return the mixture to the saucepan and heat, stirring constantly, over low heat until it thickens to coat the back of a spoon.

4. Transfer the Vanilla Sauce to a bowl and let cool. Stir in the vanilla.

Mango Sorbet

Chef Lenny De George,
Cinderella's Royal Table

Serves 4 to 6; makes about 3 cups.

End almost any meal with this light and easy-to-make sorbet.

4 large ripe mangoes, peeled, seeded, and chopped

½ cup water

2 tablespoons light corn syrup

2 tablespoons granulated sugar

1. In a blender or food processor, puree the mango; you should have about 3 cups.

2. In a bowl, stir together the mango, water, light corn syrup, and sugar until the mixture is smooth and the sugar has dissolved.

3. Chill the mixture, covered, until cold, about 2 hours.

4. Freeze in an ice cream freezer according to manufacturer's directions. Store tightly packed and covered in the freezer compartment of your refrigerator until ready to serve.

Chocolate Chip Crumbcakes

Chef Andreas Born,
Disney's BoardWalk Bakery

Makes three 3-inch by 5-inch loaves.

Enjoy this sumptuous cake with your mid-morning coffee or tea. Or serve it with a scoop of vanilla ice cream for an indulgent dessert.

1 ½ cups plus 2 tablespoons sifted cake flour

1 cup cornstarch

½ teaspoon baking powder

1 ½ cups granulated sugar

1 ¼ cups (2 ½ sticks) butter, at room temperature

1 ¼ teaspoons pure vanilla extract

½ teaspoon lemon extract

4 large eggs

1 cup semisweet chocolate chips

1. Preheat the oven to 350°F. Lightly grease and flour three 3-inch by 5-inch mini loaf pans.

2. In a medium bowl, combine 1 cup plus 2 tablespoons of the cake flour with the cornstarch and baking powder.

3. In a medium bowl, using an electric mixer, beat 1 cup sugar, 1 cup plus 2 tablespoons of the butter, ½ teaspoon vanilla, and the lemon extract for about 5 minutes, or until light and creamy. Add the eggs one at a time, beating well after each addition, and adding 2 to 3 tablespoons of the flour mixture with the last egg; the mixture may seem curdled. Beat for 3 or 4 minutes, or until creamy again.

4. With a rubber spatula, fold in the remaining flour mixture until thoroughly incorporated. Stir in the chocolate chips.

5. In a small bowl, with a fork, mix together the remaining ¼ cup sugar, 2 tablespoons butter, and ¾ teaspoon vanilla. Add the remaining ½ cup flour and mix until crumbly.

6. Fill the prepared loaf pans with the crumb cake batter and sprinkle the crumb mixture over the top. ☞

7. Bake the crumb cakes for 35 to 40 minutes, or until the middle of the cake springs back when touched lightly or a wooden pick inserted in the center comes out clean.

Disney Institute Tip: If lemon and chocolate is not your favorite flavor combination, feel free to omit the lemon extract. If you do use it, use the real thing, not an imitation extract.

Crème Brûlée

Chef Erich Herbitschek,
Disney's Grand Floridian
Resort & Spa Bakery

Serves 8.

Chef Herbitschek has perfected his version of this dessert classic, which he first learned as a young apprentice in Austria.

- **2** cups heavy cream
- **½** cup milk
- **1** cup granulated sugar plus ¼ cup for sprinkling
- **2** vanilla beans, cut in half lengthwise and seeds scraped with the tip of a sharp knife
- **6** large egg yolks

1. Preheat the oven to 250°F. In a 2-quart saucepan, bring the heavy cream, milk, sugar, the vanilla beans, and the seeds from the vanilla beans just to a boil over medium heat. Discard the vanilla beans or reserve them for another use.

2. In a bowl, whisk ½ cup of the heated cream mixture into the egg yolks, and then whisk in the remainder.

3. Pour the mixture into a 9- or 10-inch shallow glass or oven-proof baking dish. Place the baking dish in a roasting pan and fill with hot water to come halfway up the sides of the baking dish. Place the roasting pan in the oven and bake for 45 to 55 minutes, or until set. Cool to room temperature and chill, covered, for about 3 hours or overnight, until very cold.

4. When ready to serve, sprinkle the top of the custard with the remaining ¼ cup granulated sugar. Caramelize the sugar with a kitchen blowtorch or place in a roasting pan of ice water and broil, watching carefully, just until the top is caramelized.

The Wine Steward Suggests: Sauternes from Bordeaux highlight the sweet taste of Crème Brûlée.

Key Lime Pie

Chef Michael Schifano,
Olivia's Cafe

Serves 8.

Three ingredients, plus a crust you can pick up at the local supermarket, create an authentic, delectable pie. Serve with whipped cream or just by itself.

5 **large egg yolks**

One 14-ounce can sweetened condensed milk

⅔ **cup Key lime juice**

A prepared 9-inch graham cracker pie crust

1. Preheat the oven to 350°F.

2. In a bowl, gently whisk together the yolks; do not let them foam. Stirring constantly, slowly blend in the sweetened condensed milk and the lime juice.

3. Pour the mixture into the pie crust and bake for 12 to 15 minutes, or until set.

4. Remove the pie from the oven and cool to room temperature on a wire rack. Chill, covered, until very cold.

5. Serve chilled, cut into slices.

Tiramisu

Chef Erich Herbitschek, Disney's Grand Floridian Resort & Spa Bakery

Serves 12 to 16.

Make this classic Italian sweet ending to serve anytime you like.

½ cup water

½ cup plus ⅓ cup granulated sugar

¼ cup espresso coffee

¼ cup dark rum

3 cups mascarpone cheese

3 large egg yolks

2 teaspoons pure vanilla extract

2 cups heavy cream

12 Italian ladyfingers

1 tablespoon cocoa powder for serving

1. In a 2-quart saucepan, heat ½ cup water with ½ cup sugar, stirring, over medium heat, until the sugar is dissolved. Transfer the mixture to a bowl and let cool. Stir in the espresso and the dark rum.

2. In a bowl with an electric mixer, beat the mascarpone, egg yolks, ⅓ cup sugar, and vanilla until very light and smooth. Add the heavy cream and beat for 2 to 3 minutes, or until thickened.

3. Soak 5 ladyfingers in the coffee syrup and arrange them in the bottom of a 10-inch round, 4-inch deep bowl. Add a 2-inch layer of the mascarpone filling. Soak the remaining 7 ladyfingers in the coffee syrup and place on top of the mascarpone filling. Spoon in the remaining mascarpone filling and smooth the top.

4. Chill, covered, for at least 4 hours before serving. Just before serving, sprinkle the Tiramisu with cocoa powder.

The Wine Steward Suggests: Try a Vin Santo from Italy with your Tiramisu.

Bavarian Cheesecake

Chef Craig Babbony,
Biergarten Restaurant

Serves 10 to 12.

Moist, rich vanilla sponge cake is the base of this European-style cheesecake that disappears almost as soon as it's placed on the buffet in the Germany Pavilion at Epcot.

- ¾ **cup all-purpose flour**
- ¾ **teaspoon baking powder**
- ½ **teaspoon salt**
- 4 **large eggs, separated**
- 2¾ **cups granulated sugar**
- 1 **teaspoon pure vanilla extract**
- 1½ **cups heavy cream**
- 6 **ounces cream cheese**
- 6 **ounces baker's or farmer's cheese**
- 8 **ounces sour cream**
- 2 **tablespoons fresh lemon juice**
- 2 **tablespoons finely grated lemon zest**
- 1 **envelope unflavored gelatin**
- ¼ **cup water**
  Confectioners' sugar, for serving

1. Preheat the oven to 375°F. Lightly grease two 8-inch round cake pans, and line the bottoms with parchment paper.

2. Into a medium bowl, sift together the flour, baking powder, and salt.

3. In a large bowl with an electric mixer, beat 4 egg yolks and ¾ cup sugar for 4 to 5 minutes, or until very thick and lemon-colored. Add the vanilla. Gradually add the dry ingredients to the egg yolk mixture and beat just until smooth.

4. In a bowl with clean beaters, beat the egg whites just to stiff peaks. Gently fold the whites into the egg yolk mixture. Transfer the batter to the prepared cake pans and bake for 10 to 12 minutes, or until a wooden pick inserted in the center comes out clean. Cool the cakes completely on wire racks, and then invert onto the racks and remove the pans.

5. In a large bowl, whip the heavy cream just to soft peaks and set aside. In a mixing bowl, beat together the cream cheese, baker's cheese, and the remaining 2 cups granulated sugar until smooth. Add the sour cream, lemon juice, and lemon zest and beat until smooth. Gently add the whipped cream to the cheese mixture, being careful not to overbeat.

6. In a small saucepan, dissolve the gelatin in the water over very low heat. Remove the pan from the heat and let cool. With an electric mixer on medium speed, add the gelatin mixture to the cheese mixture from the edge of the bowl, being careful not to get the gelatin on the beaters or on the side of the bowl, to prevent lumping.

7. In an 8-inch springform pan lined with plastic wrap, place one of the vanilla sponge cakes smooth side down. Top with the cream mixture and place the remaining cake on top, smooth side up. Cover tightly with plastic wrap and store in the refrigerator overnight. Just before serving, remove the cake from the springform pan, remove the plastic wrap liner, and transfer the cake to a serving plate. Sprinkle confectioners' sugar across the top.

Chocolate Spice Soufflé

Chef Erich Herbitschek,
Disney's Grand Floridian
Resort & Spa Bakery

Serves 6 to 8.

Ginger, cinnamon, allspice, and nutmeg add truly distinctive, unexpected flavors to a classic chocolate soufflé.

2 tablespoons butter, softened, plus additional for soufflé dish

½ cup granulated sugar plus additional for soufflé dish

¼ cup all-purpose flour

¾ teaspoon ground ginger

¾ teaspoon ground allspice

¾ teaspoon ground cinnamon

⅛ teaspoon ground nutmeg

1 cup milk

5 large eggs

4 ounces bittersweet or semisweet (not unsweetened) chocolate, melted and cooled

1. Lightly butter and sugar a 1½-quart soufflé dish, shaking out any excess sugar.

2. In a small bowl, whisk together the flour, ginger, allspice, cinnamon, and nutmeg.

3. In a 2-quart saucepan, melt the remaining 2 tablespoons butter and stir in the flour mixture. Cook, stirring, for 1 minute. Remove the pan from the heat and add the milk, whisking constantly. Return to the heat and cook, stirring, for 2 minutes, or until the mixture boils. Cook, stirring, about 2 minutes longer, or until the batter pulls away from the side of the pan.

4. Remove the saucepan from the heat and stir in the egg yolks and the melted chocolate. Transfer to a bowl and set aside to cool completely. ☛

5. Preheat the oven to 375°F. In a bowl with an electric mixer, beat the egg whites and the remaining ½ cup sugar just to stiff peaks. Fold the egg whites into the cooled chocolate batter.

6. Transfer the cooled chocolate batter to the prepared soufflé dish; it should be about ¾ full. Bake for 15 to 20 minutes, or until well risen.

7. Serve immediately.

Artist Point Berry Cobbler

Chef Robert Adams,
Artist Point

Serves 6 to 8.

Try drizzling this cobbler with raspberry sauce just before serving, and maybe even heaping some whipped cream on the side.

1½ cups all-purpose flour

½ cup granulated sugar

2 teaspoons baking powder

½ teaspoon salt

½ cup plus 2 tablespoons cold butter, cut into small pieces

1 large egg

1 cup heavy cream

12 ounces fresh blueberries

2 tablespoons light brown sugar

½ pint each fresh raspberries and blackberries, and 8 strawberries, for garnish

1. In a medium bowl, whisk together the flour, granulated sugar, baking powder, and salt. With a pastry blender, 2 knives used scissor-style, or your hands, blend in ½ cup butter until crumbly. With a fork, stir in the egg and mix just enough to blend. Add heavy cream and mix just enough to incorporate; do not overmix.

2. Preheat the oven to 350°F. Lightly grease a 9-inch cake pan, line the bottom with wax paper, and grease the paper.

3. Press the dough evenly into the bottom of the cake pan. Place the blueberries on top of the dough and sprinkle with the brown sugar. Place the remaining 2 tablespoons butter pieces over berries.

4. Bake for 20 to 25 minutes, or until golden brown. Cool on a rack. Remove the cake from the pan, cut it in wedges, and serve it with the fresh raspberries, blackberries, and strawberries.

Victoria & Albert's Chocolate Soufflé

Chef Scott Hunnel,
Victoria & Albert's

Serves 6 to 8.

Don't be intimidated, soufflés are easy to make. Just remember, a cooked soufflé should still be soft in the center.

¼ cup (½ stick) butter plus additional for soufflé dish

¼ cup granulated sugar plus additional for soufflé dish

½ cup flour

2 cups milk

1 vanilla bean, split lengthwise

6 large eggs, separated

4 ounces bittersweet or semisweet (not unsweetened) chocolate, melted

1. Place an oven rack in the center of the oven. Place a roasting pan almost full of hot water on the rack. Preheat the oven to 350°F. Lightly butter and sugar a 1½-quart soufflé dish, shaking out any excess sugar.

2. In a 3-quart saucepan, melt ¼ cup butter over medium heat. Add the flour and cook, stirring constantly, for 2 minutes. Remove the saucepan from the heat.

3. In a 1-quart saucepan, scald the milk, ¼ cup sugar, and vanilla bean over medium-high heat. Remove the pan from the heat. Remove the vanilla bean from the milk and with a spoon, scrape out the seeds and add them to the mixture. Discard the vanilla bean.

4. Gradually add the milk mixture to the butter and flour mixture, stirring constantly to form a smooth paste. Continue stirring in any remaining milk. Return the saucepan to medium heat and cook, stirring, for about 3 minutes, or until the mixture boils and thickens. Remove the saucepan from the heat to cool slightly. ☞

5. Add 6 egg yolks, one at a time, beating well after each addition, until the mixture is smooth and glossy. Stir in the chocolate until well blended.

6. In a large bowl, with an electric mixer, beat the 6 egg whites just to stiff peaks. Whisk $\frac{1}{3}$ of the beaten egg whites into the yolk mixture until fully incorporated. Carefully fold in the remaining egg whites.

7. Fill the prepared soufflé dish and place it in the water bath. Bake for 35 to 40 minutes, or until the soufflé is well risen. Serve immediately.

Appendix

Preserved Lemons: Scrub 2 lemons and dry well. Cut each lemon into 8 wedges. In a medium bowl, toss the lemon wedges with ⅓ cup coarse salt and transfer to a glass jar. Pour in ½ cup fresh lemon juice, or more if needed. Cap the jar tightly with a glass or plastic-coated lid. Let the lemons sit at room temperature for 7 days; shake each day to distribute the salt and the lemon juice. To store, add olive oil to cover, and refrigerate. Rinse lemon wedges well before using.

Roasted Garlic: Preheat the oven to 400°F. Cut off the stem and the top third of 1 whole garlic head. Place the garlic on a sheet of heavy-duty aluminum foil and drizzle with 1 tablespoon olive oil. Wrap the garlic with foil, seal the edges tightly, and roast for 1 hour. Remove the package from the oven, open carefully, and let the garlic cool slightly. Scrape or squeeze out the pulp from the garlic cloves. You should get about 2 tablespoons roasted garlic puree from 1 head of garlic.

Ras el Hanout: In a spice grinder or a cleaned coffee grinder, grind 1 cinnamon stick, 1 tablespoon sesame seeds, 15 whole black peppercorns, 8 allspice berries, 8 whole cloves, 1 teaspoon fennel seeds, 1 teaspoon coriander seeds, the seeds from 8 cardamom pods, ½ teaspoon anise seeds, ½ teaspoon cumin seeds, and a pinch of crushed hot red pepper flakes to a fine powder. Transfer the mixture to a small bowl and stir in 1 tablespoon ground ginger, 1 teaspoon ground nutmeg, and a pinch of ground mace until well combined. Ras el hanout may be stored in a tightly closed jar in a cool dark place for up to 6 months.

Spiced Basil Oil: In a medium saucepan of boiling salted water, blanch 1 cup fresh basil leaves and ½ cup fresh spinach leaves for one minute. Drain in a sieve. In a blender, in batches if necessary, puree the basil and the spinach. Add 1 cup olive oil, 1 teaspoon green Tabasco sauce, ½ teaspoon salt, and ⅛ teaspoon freshly ground pepper and blend until well combined; the mixture should be bright green. Transfer to a bowl, cover, and let sit at room temperature for at least 24 hours. Strain the oil and discard the solids. Store any unused Spiced Basil Oil in the refrigerator.

Clear Tomato Broth: In a blender, in batches, coarsely chop 15 whole vine-ripened tomatoes with 1 teaspoon salt. Place the chopped tomatoes in a large sieve lined with a double layer of damp cheesecloth, set it over a bowl, and let the mixture drain in the refrigerator for 24 hours to collect the liquid. Discard the tomato pulp and reserve the liquid. You should have about 4 cups.

Vinaigrette Spice: In a small bowl, combine ½ teaspoon each granulated sugar, salt, and garlic powder with ¼ teaspoon each dried basil leaves, dried tarragon leaves, dried oregano leaves, dried thyme leaves, and freshly ground black pepper. Makes about 1 tablespoon.

Featured Restaurants

There are more than 250 dining spots at the Walt Disney World Resort®, with the following represented in this recipe collection:

Artist Point The fine dining spot at Disney's Wilderness Lodge offers a creative menu that features wild game as well as more traditional items such as steaks, salmon, and other Pacific seafood.

Biergarten Restaurant German yodelers, dancers, and other traditional Bavarian musicians entertain throughout the day at the Germany Pavilion at Epcot. Food is an all-you-can-eat buffet with assorted sausages, frankfurters, rotisserie chicken, homemade spaetzle, assorted cold dishes, and many more German specialties.

Boatwright's Dining Hall Cajun dishes and American home-style favorites are on the menu at Disney's Dixie Landings Resort.

Bonfamille's Cafe Steaks, seafood, and Creole cooking are the highlights at Disney's Port Orleans Resort restaurant.

California Grill This acclaimed restaurant high atop Disney's Contemporary Resort offers extraordinary cuisine with seasonal specialties (and terrific views of the Magic Kingdom fireworks).

Cape May Cafe An all-you-can-eat New England clambake is featured at this eatery at Disney's Beach Club Resort.

Captain's Tavern Prime rib, chicken, and crab legs are on the menu at Disney's Caribbean Beach Resort.

Le Cellier Steakhouse Tucked away in the Canada Pavilion at Epcot, Le Cellier offers a full menu of Canadian foods and grilled steaks.

Chef Mickey's Mickey and friends join families for a buffet-style feast on the fourth floor of Disney's Contemporary Resort.

Cinderella's Royal Table Located in Cinderella Castle in the Magic Kingdom; you'll find Cinderella and friends here much of the time. Cuisine is American—prime rib, seafood, and chicken.

Cítricos Market-fresh cuisine from the south of France varies seasonally at upscale Cítricos, located on the second floor of Disney's Grand Floridian Resort & Spa.

Concourse Steakhouse Prime rib, steaks, and burgers are the specialties at this restaurant on the fourth floor of Disney's Contemporary Resort.

Coral Reef Restaurant A panoramic view of the world's largest aquarium awaits Epcot diners, with a menu featuring fresh fish and shellfish.

Crystal Palace One of the Magic Kingdom's landmarks, guests dine in a Victorian-style garden, with Winnie the Pooh and friends visiting tables. A lavish buffet features a salad bar, deli, pasta dishes, chicken, fish, seafood, and more.

Disney's BoardWalk Bakery Fresh-baked pastries, cookies, and other goodies are lakeside on Disney's BoardWalk.

50's Prime Time Cafe The setting at the Disney-MGM Studios is straight out of your favorite sitcoms of the 1950s, and the fare is too: meatloaf, pot roast, even chicken noodle soup. There are also burgers, milkshakes, and floats.

Flame Tree Barbecue It's quick outdoor service at Disney's Animal Kingdom, with wood-roasted or smoked beef, chicken, and pork.

Flying Fish Café The cuisine at this BoardWalk eatery is creative and upscale with an emphasis on seafood and healthful options.

Garden Grill Restaurant The restaurant in The Land at Epcot revolves above scenes from the Celebrate the Land boat ride below. Mickey and Minnie join Chip 'n' Dale to host meals, including an all-you-can eat country breakfast, and rotisserie chicken, hickory-smoked steaks, and fish for lunch and dinner.

Grand Floridian Cafe Southern cooking is the specialty at this casual eatery at Disney's Grand Floridian Resort & Spa.

The Hollywood Brown Derby This is a faithful re-creation at the Disney-MGM Studios of the former Vine Street mainstay, right down to the caricatures that cover the walls. The menu features the famed Cobb Salad, tossed tableside, as well as steaks, fish, and chicken.

Narcoossee's The waterside setting at Disney's Grand Floridian Resort & Spa may be casual but the cuisine is sophisticated and market fresh, including fish, beef, and innovative vegetarian creations.

'Ohana On the second floor of Disney's Polynesian Resort, 'Ohana features a 16-foot-long open fire pit and all-you-can-eat shrimp, poultry, pork, and beef.

Olivia's Cafe Key West–inspired specialties, including Key lime pie and conch chowder, are featured at Olivia's at Disney's Old Key West Resort.

Pizzafari Gourmet pizzas are prepared in an open kitchen at this Animal Kingdom counter-service restaurant.

Restaurant Akershus Epcot's castle-like Akershus restaurant in the Norway Pavilion features a *koldtbord* (literally "cold table") with hot and cold meats and seafood and a selection of salads, cheeses, and breads.

Rose & Crown Pub & Dining Room Fish and chips and traditional meat pies are among the pub fare in the United Kingdom Pavilion at Epcot.

Seasons Fresh Florida seafood and produce are featured in this restaurant at Disney Institute.

Spoodles Noisy and fun with Mediterranean-inspired cuisine, Spoodles encourages sharing of its Greek, Spanish, Northern African, and Italian specialties. The restaurant is on Disney's BoardWalk.

Tony's Town Square Restaurant On Main Street, U.S.A., in the Magic Kingdom, Tony's décor comes straight out of the Disney film *Lady and the Tramp*. Cuisine is Italian, with grilled fish, steaks, spaghetti with meatballs, pizzas, and daily specials.

Victoria & Albert's The premier Walt Disney World restaurant at Disney's Grand Floridian Resort & Spa is the only one that requires men to wear jackets. Cuisine is Continental, with customized menus created daily.

Yacht Club Galley Informal dining at Disney's Yacht & Beach Club Resort features soups, sandwiches, and salads.

Yachtsman Steakhouse Beef is the specialty, and you can watch the butcher choosing cuts of meat in a glassed-in shop at the entrance. Vegetarian creations are also offered. The restaurant is at Disney's Yacht & Beach Club Resort.

Index

W

Y, Z